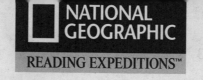

NATIONAL GEOGRAPHIC

READING EXPEDITIONS™

U0117866

国 家 地 理
科学探索丛书

SOCIAL STUDIES

社 会 科 学

World History
世界历史

TEACHER'S GUIDE & ASSESSMENTS

教师指导与评估手册

美国国家地理学会　编著

Lesson Notes

课程教案

Activity Masters

课堂活动

Teacher Resources

教学资源

外语教学与研究出版社
FOREIGN LANGUAGE TEACHING AND RESEARCH PRESS
北京　BEIJING

京权图字：01－2006－3803

"国家地理科学探索丛书·教师指导与评估手册"由美国北极星—君红传媒有限公司与外语教学与研究出版社共同策划并授权外语教学与研究出版社在中华人民共和国境内(不包括香港、澳门特别行政区及台湾省)独家出版、发行。

图书在版编目(CIP)数据

世界历史教师指导与评估手册：英文／美国国家地理学会编著 .— 北京：外语教学与研究出版社，2007.7
（国家地理科学探索丛书：注释版. 第3辑）
ISBN 978－7－5600－6022－4

Ⅰ. 世…　Ⅱ. 美…　Ⅲ. 英语—阅读教学—教学参考资料　Ⅳ. H319.4

中国版本图书馆 CIP 数据核字 (2006) 第 106812 号

出 版 人：于春迟
责任编辑：余 军
封面设计：孙莉明
出版发行：外语教学与研究出版社
社　　址：北京市西三环北路 19 号 (100089)
网　　址：http://www.fltrp.com
印　　刷：中国农业出版社印刷厂
开　　本：889×1194　1/16
印　　张：5.75
版　　次：2007 年 7 月第 1 版　2007 年 7 月第 1 次印刷
书　　号：ISBN 978－7－5600－6022－4
定　　价：11.90 元
＊　　＊　　＊
如有印刷、装订质量问题出版社负责调换
制售盗版必究　举报查实奖励
版权保护办公室举报电话：(010)88817519

Contents
目录

Lesson Notes　课程教案

Early Humans & the First Civilizations　文明的起源 ·· 10

Ancient Greece & Rome　古希腊和古罗马 ··· 30

From the Middle Ages to Renaissance　从中世纪到文艺复兴 ································· 50

Teacher Resources　教学资源

Series Overview　系列概述 ·· 4

Lesson Overview　课程概述 ·· 6

Overview of Titles　教学目标 ··· 70

Literacy Internet Resources　因特网上的资源 ·· 72

Assessment Overview　测试概述 ··· 74

Using Graphic Organizers　运用图表 ·· 83

简介 (Introduction)

"世界历史"系列介绍史前直至17世纪早期世界历史演变洪流中的重要事件、人物和地点。本系列共三本书，都以极具冲击力的视觉形式将标准科学的社会研究内容展现给大家。

- 每本书的组织方式有利于帮助学生构建阅读理解的基本框架。

- 每本书包括两大部分，每个部分开篇都对该时空特定文明的背景情况、历史年代及其在世界历史中的演进作了简要介绍，并配有一幅体现本部分主题的跨页彩图。

- 每个部分按照三大"中心思想"（Big Ideas）来组织，分别用8～9篇文章集中展开和体现，是对具体文明或历史阶段的精辟阐释。

- 每篇文章末尾设有一个"联想今日"（Why It Matters Today）版块，将讨论的话题与当今社会相联系。

- 各部分结尾的"综述"（Overview）为长约七页的参考资料，是对前文涉及的历史背景的简练总结。

本系列还富有如下几点对学生深具启发性的特色：

- "识古通今"（Past to Present）讲述过去历史中的事物与现在的关系，如奥林匹克运动会。

- "文化之间"（Across Cultures）将文章中的信息与其他文明和时代相联系，帮助学生了解所有人类文明的共性。

- "历史中的艺术"（Art in History）向学生介绍的艺术作品不仅是该时代文明的代表，也是为全世界所认可的杰作。

注重读写能力 (Focus on Literacy)

培养阅读理解技巧

本系列专为培养、锻炼和扩充学生的基本阅读技巧而设计。学生们可以运用这些阅读理解技巧学习非小说类文本特有的各种文本结构、形式和图表，如：

比较和对比 Compare and contrast	词语关联 Relate words
区分事实和观点 Distinguish fact from opinion	识别顺序 Sequence
得出结论 Draw conclusions	概括总结 Summarize
识别主题和细节 Identify main ideas and details	运用情节线索 Use context clues
识别问题和解决办法 Identify problems and solutions	作出推论 Infer
作出判断 Make judgments	运用图形辅助理解 Use images to aid comprehension
识别因果关系 Recognize cause-and-effect relationships	

理解非小说类作品的体裁、文本特征和图表

善于从非小说类作品中获得信息的读者对这类作品的各种体裁和格式都很熟悉。"世界历史"系列中涵盖了众多帮助理解非小说类作品的要素，如照片、地图、时间轴和图表；目录和注释；小标题、标注和图片说明文字。

文章对比阅读

最近关于学生阅读行为和水平的调查结果显示，让学生有机会阅读和对比多篇文章有助于提高他们的阅读技巧。本系列围绕同一个主题——不同文明的特征——组织了不同的文章，为学生提供了对比阅读的绝好机会。学生可以就如下问题展开讨论：

对比（Compare）——这几本书各自的结构是怎样的？它们之间有哪些相同点和不同点？

评价（Evaluate）——这些信息表述得是否清楚？哪些辅助手段最有用？

注重社会研究 (Focus on Science Studies)

本系列对世界历史中的以下核心概念和主题进行了解释和发展：

"早期人类"

- 旧石器时代的猎人显示出了基本的人类特征，包括制造工具、形成社会群体以及艺术创造。
- 新石器时代农民种植农作物，喂养动物，并且建造永久居住地，从而推动了人类文化的发展。
- 新的发现使考古学家不断改变或者丰富他们关于早期人类的想法。

"最早的文明"

- 美索不达米亚地区发展了文明的基本要素——写作、文学和一部法典。
- 尼罗河以及对死后生活的关注塑造了埃及文明。
- 考古学家通过研究古代的美索不达米亚地区和古埃及来了解文明的进程。

"希腊文明"

- 被地形分隔的古希腊人靠共有的生活方式联系在一起。
- 希腊文明在艺术、政治学和科学等领域创造了不朽的成就。
- 希腊传说从远古以来一直令人们倾倒。

"古罗马"

- 军事实力使罗马从一个小城邦成长为伟大的帝国。
- 罗马面临来自帝国内外的挑战。
- 罗马创造了一个强大的文明，其影响力与魅力持续至今。

"中世纪"

- 教会对中世纪社会的影响最大。
- 贸易的复兴带来了城镇的发展和一种新型的经济。
- 中世纪开始实行一些变革，这些变革后来影响了现代生活。

"文艺复兴"

- 文艺复兴始发于意大利一些富有而强大的城邦。
- 文艺复兴在文理科学中分别引发了新风格和新思想。
- 宗教改革对天主教会的变革引发了新教各派的兴起。

培养交流技巧

阅读和交流信息的能力直接关系到生活各个方面。本系列三本书的课程教案设置了很多与书中重要内容相关的写作练习。学生运用各种题材和格式进行交流表达，从而掌握写作的步骤和方法。比如：

1. 准备采访提纲（"早期人类"）
2. 运用故事结构图创作一个英雄的传说（"最早的文明"）
3. 为某历史人物写一篇讣告（"希腊文明"）
4. 写一份研究报告（"古罗马"）
5. 写一篇说明文（"中世纪"）
6. 创作一份旅游小册子（"文艺复兴"）

Lesson Overview
课程概述

课程概述 （Overview）——帮助教师快速选书备课

概要 （Summary）
此处简要概括每个部分的三大中心思想。

背景知识 (Background)
此处就书中涉及的历史阶段给出补充信息，为学生阅读提供背景知识。

学习目标 (Learning Objectives)
此处列出了非小说类作品的特点、体裁、阅读、写作以及社会研究技能等方面的重点学习目标，方便教师备课。

Overview

Early Humans & the First Civilizations
文明的起源

Early Humans 早期人类

"Early Humans" explores what scientists have learned (and continue to learn) about life in prehistoric times. The text is organized around three Big Ideas: Becoming Human; The First Farmers; and New Discoveries, New Ideas.

Summary

Becoming Human describes how making and using tools, forming social groups, and creating art set the earliest humans apart from other animals. Articles include: "Get Sharp"; "Who Were the Neandertals?"; "Really Big Game Hunters"; and "The Cave Artists."

The First Farmers explores the beginnings of agriculture, the domestication of animals, and the first cities. This section includes: "Animals Join the Family" and "At Home in Catalhuyuk."

New Discoveries, New Ideas describes the work of archaeologists and shows how new discoveries cause them to add to or change their ideas about the distant past. Articles in this section are: "What Do Archaeologists Do?"; "What Killed the Iceman?"; and "The Search for the First Americans."

Background

Prehistoric humans first appeared during the Stone Age, which began about 2.5 million years ago and lasted until the last Ice Age began, about 100,000 years ago. During the Ice Age, humans were hunters-gatherers. They lived in groups, produced art, used language, and made finely crafted tools. By the time the Ice Age ended, humans had learned to control the growth of grain crops and domesticate animals. An important effect of the planting and harvesting of crops was the development of permanent settlements. The growth of these settlements led to a division of labor, which set the stage for the first "true" civilizations.

Learning Objectives

Genre/Text Features	Reading Skills	Writing/Communication Skills	Social Studies Skills
• expository • article titles and subheads • sidebars • contents, notes and overview • maps and time lines • illustrations and photographs with captions	**Skill Focus** • identify main ideas and details • distinguish fact from opinion • use context clues **Supporting Skills** • sequence • identify cause and effect • draw conclusions	**Writing** • prepare an interview guide • write a script for a documentary • outline a mystery story **Speaking/Listening** • broadcast a TV news story	• relate the importance of technology to early humans • explain the role of art in a developing culture • identify the stages that led to the formation of early cities • interpret a time line • describe processes and tools archaeologists use

10

注重文本阅读（Focus on Content Area Reading）——关于帮助学生在阅读前后及阅读过程中培养技巧的建议

Focus on Content Area Reading

Before Reading

Activate Prior Knowledge

Refer students to the title page and write the word *human* on the board. Ask:

What does it mean to be human?
What are some characteristics that are unique to humans?

Write student responses on the board around the word *human*, creating a web. Then ask students to read pages 6-9.

Introduce the concept of prehistory and ask students how we know about the lives of early humans if they left behind no written records.

Preview

Give students a few minutes to thumb through "Early Humans" to see how it is organized. Guide students to recognize how exploring the three Big Ideas will give them insights into what it means to be human.

Point out the Overview on pages 56-62 and ask them how they might use this feature to enhance their reading.

Set Purpose

Help students to identify some practical reasons for learning about the lives of early humans. Ask:

How can the study of early humans give us a greater appreciation of the ways we live today?

Use this discussion to guide students to recognize a connection between modern and prehistoric times. Tell students that they will find other links in the Why It Matters Today feature at the end of each article.

Vocabulary Strategy: Use Context Clues

Activity Master, page 16

Refer students to the terms **prehistory** and **Ice Age** on pages 6-7.

Call on a volunteer to define each term, using context clues given in the text. Then have students complete the activity master independently and check their definitions in the notes.

Strategy Tip: Use Images to Aid Comprehension

Because the concepts of time and place may be difficult to understand, have students examine the time line on pages 6-7, the map on page 7, and the illustration of Neandertals on page 17. Discuss with students the information presented in these visuals and how they relate to the text. Make sure students understand how to extract information from visuals and captions to aid reading comprehension.

My Notes

11

阅读之前（Before Reading）

每篇文章都设置了独立的教案，并附有阅读前后和阅读过程中的练习活动。

知识热身（Activate Prior Knowledge）

这些用来热身的知识常常可以用图形工具进行组织。

词汇（Vocabulary Strategy）

学生练习理解应用课文中的关键词汇。

技巧点拨（Strategy Tip）

这些实用性提示专为提高阅读理解力设计。

注重阅读（Focus on Reading）——关于帮助学生在阅读前后及阅读过程中培养技巧的建议

预习
（Preview）

此处提供多种技巧帮助学生在阅读前把握内容。

阅读技巧
（Read Strategically）

每一种重要的阅读理解技巧都配有相应的课堂活动培养阅读能力。

课堂互动
（Respond）

此处的讨论问题可以帮助学生考查书中的主要观点。

Focus on Content Area Reading (continued)

What Do Archaeologists Do?
(pages 40–43)

Preview

Have students look at the illustrations and captions in this article to suggest answers to the title question. Challenge students to identify some of the tools archaeologists use to study prehistoric remains.

Read Strategically: Sequence

Graphic Organizer, page 85

Have students use the flow chart to sequence the steps that archaeologists follow once they have identified a site where prehistoric people were present. Then ask:

Why do you think it is important for archaeologists to follow a particular set of steps in investigating remains left by early humans?

Respond

Tell students to imagine that they are reporting from an archaeological dig on the day when the archaeologists have found an important artifact. Have students write a TV news story about this event in which they answer the questions: *Who? What? Where? When?* and *Why?*

Call on volunteers to assume the role of TV reporter and "broadcast" their story to the class.

What Killed the Iceman?
(pages 44–49)

Preview

Have students study the picture and read the text on page 44. Ask:

Who was the Iceman?

Where was he found?

Why was the discovery of the Iceman important?

Challenge them to predict how the Iceman actually died before they read the article.

Read Strategically: Identify Main Ideas and Details

Ask students to write the three text subheads from this article on a sheet of paper, leaving enough space beneath each one for notes. As they read each section, have students list facts about it. When they have finished a section, ask them to write a sentence stating the main idea and the details that support it.

Respond

Invite students to prepare an outline or synopsis for a short mystery story entitled "What Killed the Iceman?" The story, based on the article students just read, should include a setting, characters, clues, and an original solution. Encourage students to write the story as an independent project.

The Search for the First Americans (pages 50–55)

Preview

Refer students to the map on page 55 and ask them to describe what it shows. Ask:

If any of these routes are accurate, what technology did the early peo[ple] need to travel these distances?

Read Strategically: Summarize

Ask students to write this question in their notebooks.

Why have archaeologists develope[d] new ideas about when early hum[ans] reached the Western Hemisphere?

As students read the article, h[ave] them take notes that can help them answer it. When they ha[ve] finished reading, ask them to write a summary paragraph responding to the question.

Respond

Initiate a discussion to assess reading comprehension. Ask:

What are some possible routes ea[rly] humans may have taken to reach the Americas? (See map on pag[e] 55.) **(summarize)**

Why do archaeologists think tha[t] the Clovis people were in the Western Hemisphere as early as 11,500 years ago? (See page 5[3].) **(draw conclusions)**

What new evidence changed archaeologists' theories about wh[ere] and when early humans arrived [in] the Western Hemisphere? (See page 53.) **(main ideas and details)**

14

阅读之后（After Reading）——注重技能、测试和拓展活动为教学提供了丰富内容

After Reading/Assess

Focus on Skills

Investigate World History: Reading a Time Line

Activity Master, page 19

Have students use the Activity Master to analyze and interpret the time line on pages 56-57. You may want them to compare the information on this time line with that on the time line on pages 6-7.

Remind students that the time lines show a period of time before the Common Era. Explain that this period is often written B.C., because it represents the time before the presumed birth of Jesus. Point out that the years following Jesus's birth are usually written A.D.

Writing and Research: Prepare an Interview Guide

Have students choose an archaeologist identified in one of the articles to interview about his findings. Have them prepare an interview guide, identifying the topics they would like to cover—for example, biographical data about the archaeologist, what work was done at the dig site, what was found there, and the significance of the findings— and then listing questions that will give them the answers.

Ask students to exchange papers with a classmate and use the information in the selected articles to answer each other's questions. Tell students that some answers may need further research. If time permits, student pairs can role-play their interview.

Assessment Options

Questions

Use the following questions during individual conferences, or ask students to write the answers in their notebooks:

1 Why is the history of early humans called "prehistory"?

2 What uniquely human characteristics did early humans develop?

3 Who was the Iceman and how did he die?

4 What tools do archaeologists use in their work?

5 What factors led to the development of settlements such as Catalhuyuk?

6 What is the most recent theory of when and how early humans first reached the Western Hemisphere?

Assessment Activity

Have students use pictures and captions to represent each of the three Big Ideas highlighted on page 9 of this book. Students can cut pictures from magazines, create their own illustrations, or print visuals from the Internet. Remind students that each caption should not only describe the picture, but also explain how it relates to one of the Big Ideas.

Multiple-choice Test

Use the multiple-choice test on page 76.

Home-school Connection

Students and family members can look for newspaper and magazine articles as well as recently published books describing the work of archaeologists and new evidence that they have unearthed about early humans. As they review these materials, students and their families can focus on the increasingly complex accomplishments of prehistoric humans. Students should be prepared to share their ideas with the class.

Early Humans

15

注重技能（Focus on Skills）

通过有利于培养重点阅读和社会研究技能的实践活动来帮助学生通过新的方法理解书的内容。这部分也配有相关的"课堂活动"（Activity Master）。

测试（Assessment Options）

运用讨论问题、评估活动和多项选择题对学生进行评估，考查他们对书中重要概念的理解。

家庭—学校链接（Home-school Connection）

此处提供一些活动建议，让学生与家人一起讨论学到的内容。

Early Humans & the First Civilizations
文明的起源

Early Humans 早期人类

"Early Humans" explores what scientists have learned (and continue to learn) about life in prehistoric times. The text is organized around three Big Ideas: Becoming Human; The First Farmers; and New Discoveries, New Ideas.

Summary

Becoming Human describes how making and using tools, forming social groups, and creating art set the earliest humans apart from other animals. Articles include: "Get Sharp"; "Who Were the Neandertals?"; "Really Big Game Hunters"; and "The Cave Artists."

The First Farmers explores the beginnings of agriculture, the domestication of animals, and the first cities. This section includes: "Animals Join the Family" and "At Home in Catalhuyuk."

New Discoveries, New Ideas describes the work of archaeologists and shows how new discoveries cause them to add to or change their ideas about the distant past. Articles in this section are: "What Do Archaeologists Do?"; "What Killed the Iceman?"; and "The Search for the First Americans."

Background

Prehistoric humans first appeared during the Stone Age, which began about 2.5 million years ago and lasted until the last Ice Age began, about 100,000 years ago. During the Ice Age, humans were hunters-gatherers. They lived in groups, produced art, used language, and made finely crafted tools. By the time the Ice Age ended, humans had learned to control the growth of grain crops and domesticate animals. An important effect of the planting and harvesting of crops was the development of permanent settlements. The growth of these settlements led to a division of labor, which set the stage for the first "true" civilizations.

Learning Objectives

Genre/Text Features

- expository
- article titles and subheads
- sidebars
- contents, notes and overview
- maps and time lines
- illustrations and photographs with captions

Reading Skills

Skill Focus
- identify main ideas and details
- distinguish fact from opinion
- use context clues

Supporting Skills
- sequence
- identify cause and effect
- draw conclusions

Writing/Communication Skills

Writing
- prepare an interview guide
- write a script for a documentary
- outline a mystery story

Speaking/Listening
- broadcast a TV news story

Social Studies Skills

- relate the importance of technology to early humans
- explain the role of art in a developing culture
- identify the stages that led to the formation of early cities
- interpret a time line
- describe processes and tools archaeologists use

Focus on Content Area Reading

Before Reading

Activate Prior Knowledge

Refer students to the title page and write the word *human* on the board. Ask:

What does it mean to be human?

What are some characteristics that are unique to humans?

Write student responses on the board around the word *human*, creating a web. Then ask students to read pages 6-9.

Introduce the concept of prehistory and ask students how we know about the lives of early humans if they left behind no written records.

Preview

Give students a few minutes to thumb through "Early Humans" to see how it is organized. Guide students to recognize how exploring the three Big Ideas will give them insights into what it means to be human.

Point out the Overview on pages 56-62 and ask them how they might use this feature to enhance their reading.

Set Purpose

Help students to identify some practical reasons for learning about the lives of early humans. Ask:

How can the study of early humans give us a greater appreciation of the ways we live today?

Use this discussion to guide students to recognize a connection between modern and prehistoric times. Tell students that they will find other links in the Why It Matters Today feature at the end of each article.

Vocabulary Strategy: Use Context Clues

Activity Master, page 16

Refer students to the terms **prehistory** and **Ice Age** on pages 6-7.

Call on a volunteer to define each term, using context clues given in the text. Then have students complete the activity master independently and check their definitions in the notes.

Strategy Tip: Use Images to Aid Comprehension

Because the concepts of time and place may be difficult to understand, have students examine the time line on pages 6-7, the map on page 7, and the illustration of Neandertals on page 17. Discuss with students the information presented in these visuals and how they relate to the text. Make sure students understand how to extract information from visuals and captions to aid reading comprehension.

My Notes

Get Sharp
(pages 10–13)

Preview

Have students read the introductory words and the first paragraph on page 10. Discuss some of the tools students use today. Then ask:

In general, what are the purposes of tools?
Why would early humans want to make and use tools?

Explain that in this article, students will explore how the use of tools helped early humans to survive.

Read Strategically: Sequence
Graphic Organizer, page 85

Distribute copies of the flow chart. Have students use it to track the stages in the development of toolmaking.

Respond

Initiate a discussion to assess reading comprehension. Ask:

What were two results of using tools for hunting? (See page 13.) **(cause and effect)**

How does toolmaking set humans apart from other animals? (See pages 10–13.) **(draw conclusions)**

What are some tools that people use today that can be traced back to Stone Age hunters? (See pages 12–13.) **(main ideas and details)**

Who Were the Neandertals?
(pages 14–19)

Preview

Ask students to share their impressions of early humans such as the Neandertals. Have students scan the article, reading the introductory words and looking at the photos and their captions to get a sense of how ideas about the Neandertals continue to change. Ask:

What evidence helps explain our views of Neandertals?

Tell students that in this article they will explore what scientists have learned about the Neandertals.

Read Strategically: Identify Main Ideas and Details
Activity Master, page 17

As students read the article, have them think about the main ideas or important concepts in the article, and the details or important facts that support the main ideas. Then have students read the five statements on the Activity Master and follow the directions to help clarify the differences between main ideas and details.

Respond

Have students reread the article and take notes on what they find most interesting or distinctive about the Neandertals. Ask them to use their notes to write a descriptive paragraph, poem, or rap about the Neandertals.

Really Big Game Hunters
(pages 20–23)

Preview

Ask students what the word *game* means as it is used in the title of the article. If necessary, explain that *game* refers to wild animals, fish or birds that are hunted for food or sometimes for sport. Tell students to look at the picture on pages 20–21 and identify what game this article will describe.

Read Strategically: Identify Details

Have students write these two main ideas in their notebooks.

Early humans learned to work together to hunt and kill woolly mammoths.

Early humans learned to use every part of a dead woolly mammoth.

As students read the article, ask them to write details supporting each main idea.

Respond

Tell students to imagine that they have been asked to create a full-page advertisement to attract Ice Age hunters to join in a woolly mammoth hunt. Ask students to identify ways in which this huge mammal, once killed, can make life more comfortable for the hunters. Encourage students to design their own ads as an independent project.

The Cave Artists
(pages 24-29)

Preview

Give students a few minutes to skim the article. Ask:

Why do you think these cave paintings are so important in the study of early humans?

Have students read the article to check their answers.

Read Strategically: Draw Conclusions

Write the following on the board:

What do the cave paintings reveal about the people who created them?

As they read the article, have students take notes that will help them answer the question. When they have finished reading, ask them to list conclusions they can draw about early humans based on their paintings. Remind students that when they draw conclusions, they combine information they read with what they know to come up with a logical response.

Respond

Ask students to imagine they are writing the script for a documentary film about the caves at Lascaux. Have them work in small groups to create a script (or storyboards) explaining: (1) *how the cave paintings were discovered;* (2) *what the pictures show;* (3) *techniques the artists used;* and (4) *the historical significance of the paintings.*

Animals Join the Family
(pages 30–33)

Preview

Write the terms *wild animals* and *domestic animals* on the board. Ask students to define these terms and give examples. Have students read page 31 and ask:

Why was the taming of wild animals such a significant achievement for early humans?

Have students read the article to find out how domesticating animals changed the lives of early humans.

Read Strategically: Recognize Cause-and-effect Relationships
Graphic Organizer, page 87

Ask students to fill in the following causes on the graphic organizer:

Humans developed a relationship with dogs.
Early farmers domesticated wild sheep, goats and cattle.
Farmers tamed horses, donkeys and camels.

As students read the article, have them fill in the effects of each cause. Encourage them to add any other causes and effects described in the article.

Respond

Have students select three photographs in this article and use information in the text to write a new caption for each photo.

At Home in Catalhuyuk
(pages 34–39)

Preview

Discuss with students why cities are important to civilizations. Ask students to speculate on what the first cities might have been like, how they might have developed, and how these places affected the lives of early humans who lived there.

Read Strategically: Distinguish Fact from Opinion
Activity Master, page 18

As students read the article, have them use the Activity Master as a study guide to help them distinguish fact from opinion. Remind them that facts can be proven true or false, while opinions state beliefs or feelings.

Respond

Initiate a class discussion to assess reading comprehension. Ask:

What was daily life like for the people who lived in Catalhuyuk? (See pages 36 and 39.) **(summarize)**

What led to the division of labor among the people who lived in this early town? (See page 39.) **(cause and effect)**

What were the advantages of the location of Catalhuyuk? (See page 39.) **(draw conclusions)**

What Do Archaeologists Do?
(pages 40–43)

Preview

Have students look at the illustrations and captions in this article to suggest answers to the title question. Challenge students to identify some of the tools archaeologists use to study prehistoric remains.

Read Strategically: Sequence

Graphic Organizer, page 85

Have students use the flow chart to sequence the steps that archaeologists follow once they have identified a site where prehistoric people were present. Then ask:

Why do you think it is important for archaeologists to follow a particular set of steps in investigating remains left by early humans?

Respond

Tell students to imagine that they are reporting from an archaeological dig on the day when the archaeologists have found an important artifact. Have students write a TV news story about this event in which they answer the questions: *Who? What? Where? When?* and *Why?*

Call on volunteers to assume the role of TV reporter and "broadcast" their story to the class.

What Killed the Iceman?
(pages 44–49)

Preview

Have students study the picture and read the text on page 44. Ask:

Who was the Iceman?

Where was he found?

Why was the discovery of the Iceman important?

Challenge them to predict how the Iceman actually died before they read the article.

Read Strategically: Identify Main Ideas and Details

Ask students to write the three text subheads from this article on a sheet of paper, leaving enough space beneath each one for notes. As they read each section, have students list facts about it. When they have finished a section, ask them to write a sentence stating the main idea and the details that support it.

Respond

Invite students to prepare an outline or synopsis for a short mystery story entitled "What Killed the Iceman?" The story, based on the article students just read, should include a setting, characters, clues, and an original solution. Encourage students to write the story as an independent project.

The Search for the First Americans
(pages 50–55)

Preview

Refer students to the map on page 55 and ask them to describe what it shows. Ask:

If any of these routes are accurate, what technology did the early people need to travel these distances?

Read Strategically: Summarize

Ask students to write this question in their notebooks.

Why have archaeologists developed new ideas about when early humans reached the Western Hemisphere?

As students read the article, have them take notes that can help them answer it. When they have finished reading, ask them to write a summary paragraph responding to the question.

Respond

Initiate a discussion to assess reading comprehension. Ask:

What are some possible routes early humans may have taken to reach the Americas? (See map on page 55.) **(summarize)**

Why do archaeologists think that the Clovis people were in the Western Hemisphere as early as 11,500 years ago? (See page 52.) **(draw conclusions)**

What new evidence changed archaeologists' theories about where and when early humans arrived in the Western Hemisphere? (See page 53.) **(main ideas and details)**

Focus on Skills

 Investigate World History: Reading a Time Line

Activity Master, page 19

Have students use the Activity Master to analyze and interpret the time line on pages 56-57. You may want them to compare the information on this time line with that on the time line on pages 6-7.

Remind students that the time lines show a period of time before the Common Era. Explain that this period is often written B.C., because it represents the time before the presumed birth of Jesus. Point out that the years following Jesus's birth are usually written A.D.

Writing and Research: Prepare an Interview Guide

Have students choose an archaeologist identified in one of the articles to interview about his findings. Have them prepare an interview guide, identifying the topics they would like to cover—for example, biographical data about the archaeologist, what work was done at the dig site, what was found there, and the significance of the findings—and then listing questions that will give them the answers.

Ask students to exchange papers with a classmate and use the information in the selected articles to answer each other's questions. Tell students that some answers may need further research. If time permits, student pairs can role-play their interview.

Assessment Options

Questions

Use the following questions during individual conferences, or ask students to write the answers in their notebooks:

1 Why is the history of early humans called "prehistory"?

2 What uniquely human characteristics did early humans develop?

3 Who was the Iceman and how did he die?

4 What tools do archaeologists use in their work?

5 What factors led to the development of settlements such as Catalhuyuk?

6 What is the most recent theory of when and how early humans first reached the Western Hemisphere?

Assessment Activity

Have students use pictures and captions to represent each of the three Big Ideas highlighted on page 9 of this book. Students can cut pictures from magazines, create their own illustrations, or print visuals from the Internet. Remind students that each caption should not only describe the picture, but also explain how it relates to one of the Big Ideas.

Multiple-choice Test

Use the multiple-choice test on page 76.

Home-school Connection

Students and family members can look for newspaper and magazine articles as well as recently published books describing the work of archaeologists and new evidence that they have unearthed about early humans. As they review these materials, students and their families can focus on the increasingly complex accomplishments of prehistoric humans. Students should be prepared to share their ideas with the class.

Vocabulary: Use Context Clues

When you do not know what a term means, you can often use the context, the words that come before or after the unknown term, to figure out its meaning. Circle the words in each sentence that help you determine the meaning of the term in italics. Write what you think the term means. Then check your definition against the definition in the notes of the text and the dictionary.

1. Because writing had not yet been invented, scientists must study the remains left by early humans to learn about *prehistory.*

Meaning from context: _____

2. *Archaeologists,* people who study the remains of prehistoric times, often begin by identifying a place where prehistoric people were present.

Meaning from context: _____

3. Early farmers were the first to *domesticate* and raise wild animals such as the ancestors of dogs, goats and sheep.

Meaning from context: _____

4. Much of what is today Arctic Russia was the *habitat* of an elephant-type animal that could survive the cold climate.

Meaning from context: _____

5. The scientists began to *excavate* by carefully removing layers of soil from the site.

Meaning from context: _____

6. Many people living in the first cities became *artisans,* such as potters, weavers and carpenters.

Meaning from context: _____

7. The *Neolithic Age* is a much shorter period of time than the Old Stone or Paleolithic Age which began 2.5 million years ago.

Meaning from context: _____

8. The earliest forms of *technology* were stone tools and weapons created by early humans.

Meaning from context: _____

Read Strategically: Identify Main Ideas and Details

The main ideas of an article are what the article is mostly about. Details are facts and examples that explain and support each main idea. Finish the chart below with details that support each main idea from the article "Who Were the Neandertals?"

1. Main Idea:	The Neandertals had to adapt to survive in the cold climate of a harsh, frozen wilderness.
Details	
•	
•	

2. Main Idea:	Although they had only simple weapons, Neandertals learned to go after larger animals that were difficult to kill.
Details	
•	
•	

3. Main Idea:	Some Neandertal behaviors show signs of an organized society.
Details	
•	
•	

4. Main Idea:	Some scientists believe that Cro-Magnon people were responsible for the disappearance of the Neandertals.
Details	
•	
•	

5. Main Idea:	Using computer technology, it appears that the faces of Neandertals were very different from the faces of modern humans.
Details	
•	
•	

Read Strategically: Distinguish Fact from Opinion

In "At Home in Catalhuyuk," you will read about the development of a town during Neolithic times. For each topic covered in the article, write one fact and one opinion. The first is done for you.

1. **Topic:** Appearance of Catalhuyuk

   Fact <u>Archaeologists have been excavating Catalhuyuk for many years to learn about this early city.</u>

   Opinion <u>The town of Catalhuyuk looks strange to modern eyes.</u>

2. **Topic:** Importance of location of Catalhuyuk

   Fact _____

   Opinion _____

3. **Topic:** Value of certain crops

   Fact _____

   Opinion _____

4. **Topic:** Work of artisans

   Fact _____

   Opinion _____

5. **Topic:** Role of religion

   Fact _____

   Opinion _____

6. **Topic:** Development of trade

   Fact _____

   Opinion _____

Investigate World History: Reading a Time Line

The time line on pages 56-57 of "Early Humans" can help you keep track of some of the major events that took place during the Stone Age. Study the time line carefully. Then complete the activities that follow.

1. What is the earliest date on the time line?_____

What is the latest date? _____

2. About when did the first towns appear? _____

3. Which occurred first: the appearance of Cro-Magnons, or the disappearance of Neandertals?

_____

4. About how many years passed between the first farmers and the first towns?

_____

5. About when did humans begin making bronze tools?

_____

6. Why are there arrows at both ends of the time line?

_____

7. About when did early humans begin making stone tools?

_____

_____

8. According to the time line, what were some accomplishments of early humans?

_____

_____

_____

The First Civilizations
最早的文明

"The First Civilizations" explores what archaeologists have learned about the first civilizations in Mesopotamia and Egypt. The text looks at three Big Ideas: The Rise of Civilization; Life and Death in Egypt; and The Lure of the Past.

Summary

The Rise of Civilization examines the basic features of a civilization: written language, literature, and a code of laws. Articles in this section include: "Cracking the Code"; "Schools for Scribes"; "A Hero's Quest"; and "'A Tooth for a Tooth'."

Life and Death in Egypt describes the relationship of Egyptian civilization to the Nile River as well as the Egyptians' belief in the afterlife. Articles include: "The Gifts of the Nile"; "The Pyramid Builders"; and "Journey to the Afterlife."

The Lure of the Past describes how archaeologists work and what they have learned about the social and cultural development of ancient Egypt and Mesopotamia. In this section are: "Riches from the Tombs of Ur"; "Digging Up the Past"; and "The Mummy Hunter and Mr. X."

Background

The earliest civilizations appeared around 3500 B.C. in Mesopotamia, the region between the Tigris and Euphrates Rivers (present-day Iraq). Mesopotamia was a natural place to settle because of its rich lands and abundant water supply. Farming villages in southern Mesopotamia gave rise to the first civilization, Sumer. Sumerian civilization was characterized by government, written records, art and literature. At about the same time cities appeared in Sumer, the ancient Egyptian civilization was developing in the Nile River Valley, a fertile region with abundant water. The Nile River was also an important transportation route, linking northern and southern Egypt. The Egyptians were also unified by their religion, particularly their belief in the afterlife.

Learning Objectives

Genre/Text Features

- expository
- article titles and subheads
- contents, overview and notes
- maps and time lines
- photographs and illustrations with captions

Reading Skills

Skill Focus
- identify problems and solutions
- distinguish fact from opinion
- relate words

Supporting Skills
- recognize cause and effect
- identify main ideas and details
- sequence
- draw conclusions

Writing/Communication Skills

Writing
- write an original epic
- write a diary entry

Speaking/Listening
- present a skit
- role-play an interview
- debate a topic

Social Studies Skills

- identify and locate the Fertile Crescent
- name the basic features of a civilization and cite examples from Sumerian and ancient Egyptian civilizations
- identify the relationship between growth of civilizations and geographical features
- explain how archaeologists study the past

Focus on Content Area Reading

Before Reading

Activate Prior Knowledge

Refer students to the opening spread on pages 64-65 and have them read the title and introductory paragraph. Write *civilization* on the board and ask students to name some characteristics of a civilization. Then have students read pages 66-69 and add any other characteristics to their answers. Note that the three Big Ideas highlighted on pages 68-69 will help them understand the features of a civilization.

Preview

Give students a few minutes to look through "The First Civilizations." Urge them to pay particular attention to the table of contents, introductory paragraphs, Why It Matters Today feature, and selected graphic aids. Call attention to the Overview on pages 118-122. A time line on pages 118-119 shows the order of events between 3000 B.C.–1075 B.C.

Ask:

How is "The First Civilizations" organized?

How might you use the visuals to help you better understand the text?

Set Purpose

Ask students to think of instances today in which geography plays an important role in the development of a nation or a culture. Direct students to the map on page 67 and ask:

What geographical features might affect the development of Mesopotamia and ancient Egypt?

In what ways do you predict that these two civilizations will be similar?

Have students decide what they want to learn about these early civilizations.

Vocabulary Strategy: Relate Words

Graphic Organizer, page 90

Explain to students that many of the vocabulary words they will be using relate to a particular topic. Distribute the concept web and have students write *Written Communication* in the center circle. Then, have students use the notes in the text to fill in each circle with a word related to *Written Communication* and a definition.

Strategy Tip: Make Predictions

Remind students that making predictions or informed guesses about an article before they read it can help to focus their reading. Students can preview text features, such as headings and visuals, to make predictions and read to confirm or modify them.

My Notes

Cracking the Code
(pages 70–75)

Preview

Give students time to look through this article, paying particular attention to the photographs and captions. Ask students to predict the meaning of the title and suggest reasons why cracking a code would be important in the study of early civilizations. Have students read the article to confirm or modify their responses.

Read Strategically: Identify Main Ideas and Details

Ask students to write *Cracking the Code* followed by the two text subheads in this article on a sheet of paper. As they read each section, have them list facts about it. When students have completed their note-taking, ask them to write a paragraph stating three main ideas in this article and two details that support each.

Respond

Have pairs of students devise a simple set of pictogram symbols. Ask them to use the symbols to write a brief message. When everyone has finished, have pairs exchange their messages and try to crack the code. Discuss why writing is an important feature in a civilization and the kinds of information that can be uncovered by reading ancient writings.

Schools for Scribes
(pages 76–79)

Preview

Call attention to the picture on pages 76–77 and the title of this article. Have students infer the meaning of the word *scribe*. Point out that *scribe* comes from the Latin word *scribere*, which means "to write."

Read Strategically: Recognize Cause-and-effect Relationships
Graphic Organizer, page 87

Have students write each of the following causes in a box on the Activity Master:

Learning to write in Sumer was difficult.

As Sumerian cities grew, more recordkeeping was needed.

Student scribes had much to learn.

Women priests kept temple records.

Tell students to write an effect for each cause and then write their own cause-effect statement.

Respond

Have students work in small groups to prepare a script for a play called "Scribe School Days." The play should be set in a tablet house in Sumer and include parts for both teachers and students. Encourage students to use information from this article as well as their own classroom experiences. Set aside time for groups to present their plays.

A Hero's Quest
(pages 80–83)

Preview

Have students read the title of this article and the first sentence on page 81. Discuss the meaning of the terms *epic* and *quest*, emphasizing that most epics tell about a hero and his adventures in search of something very difficult to obtain. Ask students to name and tell about some other epics with which they are familiar.

Read Strategically: Sequence Events

As students read the article independently, have them list the most important events in the life of Gilgamesh in the correct sequence.

Respond: Write an Epic
Activity Master, page 29

Have students work independently or with a partner to create their own epic about a hero of their choice. Students can use the story map on the Activity Master to organize their ideas before writing. Provide time for students to share their heroic tales, or a synopsis of their story, with the rest of the class.

"A Tooth for a Tooth"
(pages 84–87)

Preview

Direct students to the picture and its caption on pages 84-85. Ask how the picture shows that:

Hammurabi was the head of an organized government.

The arts flourished in this early Mesopotamian civilization.

Ask students to tell what they think the title means.

Read Strategically: Summarize

Ask students to write this question in their notebooks:

What were the major purposes of Hammurabi's Code?

As students read the article, have them take notes that will help them identify the reasons Hammurabi created the code of laws. When they have finished reading, ask them to write a short summary of the article that answers the question.

Respond

Organize the class into two teams to debate the issue: "Let the punishment fit the crime." The class should set up rules for the debate, such as how many speakers should speak for each side. Students on each team should work together to prepare notes to support their point of view. Allow time for students to debate the topic.

The Gifts of the Nile
(pages 88–91)

Preview

Give students time to study the photograph on pages 88-89. Ask:

From the photo, how do you think the Egyptians used the waters of the Nile?

Read Strategically: Draw Conclusions

Ask students to list the "gifts of the Nile" as they read the article. Then have them draw conclusions about how the Nile River helped to shape the civilization of ancient Egypt. Explain that when you draw a conclusion, you make a decision about something based on the information you are given and what you already know.

Respond

Initiate a class discussion to assess reading comprehension. Ask:

Why did the Nile Valley become one of the most important food-producers in the ancient world? (See page 90.) **(cause and effect)**

How did the Nile help to unify and organize Egyptian society? (See pages 90-91.) **(draw conclusions)**

What is the relationship between the Nile and Osiris? (See page 91.) **(make connections)**

The Pyramid Builders
(pages 92–99)

Preview

Have students study the photograph and its caption and read the introductory paragraph on pages 92-93. Ask:

Why do you think the pyramids are among the greatest achievements of ancient Egyptian civilization?

Encourage students to recall some of the characteristics of a civilization—such as art, religion, government—and relate each to these colossal structures. Direct students to the art feature on pages 98-99. Ask them to think about how art reflects the values of a civilization or nation as they read.

Read Strategically: Identify Problems and Solutions
Activity Master, page 26

Explain that although the pyramids are spectacular structures, building them posed many problems. As they read, have students use the Activity Master to identify problems and solutions in pyramid building.

Respond

Tell students to imagine they are workers or overseers helping to build the pyramids at Giza. Ask them to write a diary entry describing activities at the work site and at home in a newly-built village nearby. Encourage students to use the text as well as research from books and the Internet.

Journey to the Afterlife
(pages 100–105)

Preview

Ask students to read the introductory paragraph on page 100. Invite them to predict the kinds of preparations the Egyptians made for their journey to the afterlife. Discuss how this interest in death and the afterlife relate to the characteristics of civilization.

Read Strategically: Make Judgments

Graphic Organizer, page 88

Have students use the KWL chart as a guide to reading this article. Before reading, have them fill in what they already know about Egyptian beliefs about and preparations for death, and what they want to learn. As they read, have them fill in facts they have learned. When they have finished, ask them to write a paragraph telling what they found most interesting in the article.

Respond

To assess comprehension, ask:

What preparations were made for the death of a pharaoh before he died? After his death? (See pages 102–105.) **(summarize)**

Which preparations were the most important? Why? (See page 104.) **(draw conclusions)**

What steps did embalmers follow to make a mummy? (See pages 104–105.) **(sequence)**

Riches from the Tombs of Ur
(pages 106–109)

Preview

Help students recall the pharaohs' preparations for death and their burials. Have students read the article title and look at the photographs. Invite them to predict what they will read about in this article. Call on a volunteer to locate Ur on a world map.

Read Strategically: Identify Main Ideas and Details

Graphic Organizer, page 89

Have students use the graphic organizer to help them identify the main ideas of the article. Remind students that to find main ideas, they should ask themselves what the article is mainly about. To find details that support those ideas, they should find facts or examples that show the main ideas are true.

Respond

Invite students to imagine that their city or town has hired them to create a poster to advertise an upcoming exhibit, "The Treasures of Ur" at the local museum. Have students review the article for ideas for their poster. Encourage them to create illustrations and text to make the exhibit sound exciting. Encourage students to find additional information about the tombs of Ur at http://oi.uchicago.edu/OI/UR. Click on any of the topics listed, such as jewelry, art and metal objects.

Digging Up the Past
(pages 110–113)

Preview

Refer students to the title of this article and the terms *archaeology*, *archaeologist*, and *field work* in the first sentence on page 110. Encourage students to use context clues to define these terms. Then explain that in this article, students will learn what an archaeologist does.

Read Strategically: Synthesize

Tell students to look for qualifications and skills needed to be an archaeologist as they read the interview. Then have them use their notes to write a classified ad for an archaeologist to join a team doing field work in the Middle East.

Respond

Have students work in pairs to prepare questions for an interview with an archaeologist. The purpose of the interview should be to learn how the archaeologist works and what he or she has discovered in Mesopotamia or ancient Egypt. Students should use information from the text as well as other resources to help them write questions. Pairs of students can role-play the interview, with one student asking the questions and the other answering them.

The Mummy Hunter & Mr. X (pages 115–117)

Preview

Have students read the first paragraph on page 115. Ask students to cite reasons why Egyptian mummies continue to fascinate people today.

Read Strategically: Distinguish Fact from Opinion

Activity Master, page 27

Have students use the topics listed on the Activity Master to guide them toward certain main ideas in the article. When they have finished reading, ask them to return to these topics and state one fact and one opinion about each. Remind them that facts can be proved, while opinions are beliefs or feelings.

Respond

Initiate a class discussion to assess reading comprehension. Ask:

How did the mummies of Bahariya differ from other Egyptian mummies? (See page 116.) **(compare and contrast)**

What did X-rays reveal about Mr. X? (See page 117.)

(summarize)

Why do you think much still remains to be done by future mummy hunters? **(draw conclusions)**

Focus on Skills

Investigate World History: Locating the First Civilizations

Activity Master, page 28
Have students locate and label significant places in ancient Mesopotamia and Egypt and then use the map to explain how geography affected the development of the first civilizations.

Assessment Options

Questions

Use the following questions during individual conferences, or ask students to write their answers in their notebooks:

1 Why did cities develop in the Fertile Crescent and the Nile Valley?

2 How was cuneiform used in the ancient Middle East?

3 What were the purposes of Hammurabi's Code?

4 How did the Egyptians prepare for death?

5 What can technology such as X-rays reveal about life in Mesopotamia and ancient Egypt?

Assessment Activity

Have students work alone or in pairs to create brochures for a particular location in Mesopotamia or ancient Egypt such as a tablet school at Sumer, the pyramids at Giza, or the tombs at Bahariya.

The brochures should include:

✓ an overview of the location/attraction

✓ a paragraph describing what makes this place/attraction special

✓ a map of the Middle East with a marker showing where the place is

Encourage students to use data from the text as well as from other resources.

Multiple-choice Test

Use the multiple-choice test on page 77.

Home-school Connection

Students can share the story of Gilgamesh with their families. Students and family members can then discuss other legends or folklore that the parents or other adults may have heard of. Stories can be about people, animals, places, or events. Students and their families can talk about how such legends start and why people might tell them.

Read Strategically: Identify Problems and Solutions

As you read "The Pyramid Builders," you will discover problems that faced the people who built the pyramids. You will also explore solutions to those problems. After each problem below, write a solution described in the text.

1. Problem: The Great Pyramid of Giza contained some blocks that weighed about 50 tons each.

Solution: _____

_____

2. Problem: Many of the stones that formed the pyramid had to be raised to great heights.

Solution: _____

_____

3. Problem: To complete the pyramid in 20 years, workers had to set one block in place every few minutes.

Solution: _____

_____

4. Problem: Full-time workers needed some sort of home life when they were not working.

Solution: _____

_____

5. Problem: Workers could not afford to have their bodies mummified or to be buried in ornate tombs.

Solution: _____

_____

6. Problem: Some workers became ill with various diseases.

Solution: _____

_____

7. Problem: Some workers may have had lands to farm and could not work all year round.

Solution: _____

_____

Read Strategically: Distinguish Fact from Opinion

In "The Mummy Hunter & Mr. X," you read about Dr. Zahi Hawass and his work with mummies. For each topic covered in the article, write one fact and one opinion. Remember that a statement of fact can be proved true or false. An opinion describes feelings or beliefs about something.

1. Topic: Town of Bahariya

Fact _____

Opinion _____

_____

2. Topic: Death and burial of Mr. X

Fact _____

Opinion _____

_____

3. Topic: Moving Mr. X to the lab

Fact _____

Opinion _____

_____

4. Topic: What X-rays revealed about Mr. X

Fact _____

Opinion _____

_____

5. Topic: A career as a mummy hunter

Fact _____

Opinion _____

_____

Investigate World History: Locating the First Civilizations

Use the map on page 67 to complete the activities below.

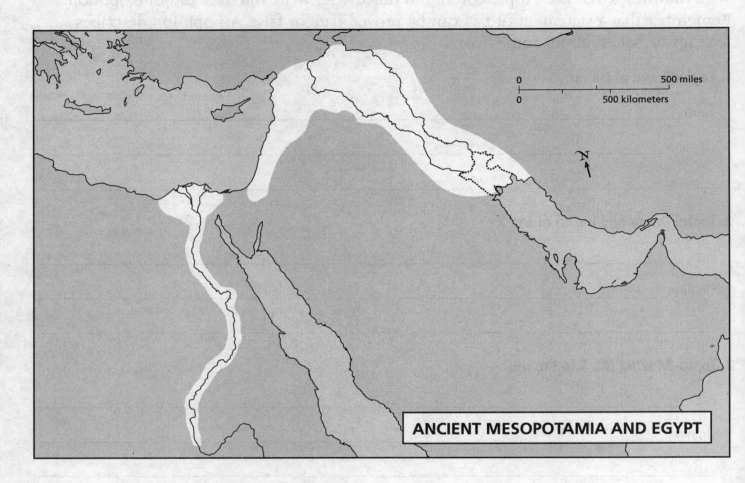

ANCIENT MESOPOTAMIA AND EGYPT

1. Use a color pen or pencil to show and label ancient Egypt.

2. Use a 2nd color to show and label the Fertile Crescent.

3. Label Mesopotamia and Sumer.

4. Label the Red Sea, Mediterranean Sea and Persian Gulf.

5. Label the Nile, Tigris and Euphrates Rivers.

Write a caption to go with the map. In your caption, explain how geographic features in this region affected the growth and development of the first civilizations.

_____

_____

Prewriting: Write an Epic

You will be writing an original epic that has the same features as those you read about in "A Hero's Quest." Your hero can be any character you admire—from history, adventure stories, the movies, or from real life. Plan your story by filling in the story map below.

Historical Setting (Time/Place)   **Character (Narrator/Other Characters)**

Problem/Goal

Events/Action

Ending/Solution

Ancient Greece & Rome

古希腊和古罗马

Greek Civilization

希腊文明

"Greek Civilization" describes the features and achievements of Greek civilization. The contents are organized around three Big Ideas: A Shared Culture; Legacy of Ancient Greece; and The Power of Legend.

Summary

A Shared Culture examines aspects of Greek life that united the ancient Greeks. Articles include: "Down to the Sea in Ships"; "Going to the Games"; and "A Visit to Delphi."

Legacy of Ancient Greece compares life in Athens and Sparta and highlights the achievements of Athens during its Golden Age particularly, in politics, science and the arts. Articles include: "The Great Rivals"; "The Parthenon: Home for a Goddess"; "The Power of the People"; and "Problem Solvers."

The Power of Legend explores how the history of ancient Greece lives on in its legends and stories. Articles include: "In Search of Troy" and "Alexander the Great."

Background

The period of Greek history from 1250 B.C. to 300 B.C. saw the rise of Athens and Sparta with their opposing philosophies of government and society. Sparta, which focused on military power and rigid class structure, is remembered primarily for its wars. Athens, with its ideas of democracy and creativity, left a legacy of rich mythology, classical architecture and philosophy, and significant advances in mathematics and science. This Greek legacy remains a powerful influence on the world today.

For additional historical background, see the Overview on pages 56-62.

Learning Objectives

Genre/Text Features
- expository
- article titles and subheads
- illustrations and photographs with captions
- maps and time lines
- contents, notes and overview
- sidebars

Reading Skills

Skill Focus
- compare and contrast
- make generalizations
- use word origins

Supporting Skills
- recognize cause-and-effect relationships
- identify main ideas and details
- summarize
- draw conclusions

Writing/Communication Skills

Writing
- create a myth
- write an obituary for a historical figure
- take notes for a TV script

Speaking/Listening
- debate an issue
- read aloud

Social Studies Skills
- explain effects of geography on a civilization
- compare the cultures of Athens and Sparta
- identify democratic features of Athenian government
- describe some classical features of Greek architecture
- use a primary source
- map the conquests of Alexander the Great

Focus on Content Area Reading

Before Reading

Activate Prior Knowledge

Ask students to look at the picture on pages 4-5 and tell how this image relates to ancient Greek Civilization. Call on volunteers to identify people, places and events they connect to ancient Greece. Record their responses in a three-column chart with columns labeled "Culture," "People" and "Events." Encourage students to add to the chart as they read.

Preview

Give students a few minutes to thumb through "Greek Civilization" and see how it is organized. Guide them to note different features: the Big Ideas, Why It Matters Today, photos and captions, time lines, and the Overview. Ask:

How is "Greek Civilization" organized?
What other features might be helpful as you read each article?

Set Purpose

Engage students in a class discussion of what they might learn about their own culture from studying ancient cultures. Point out that the three Big Ideas highlighted on pages 8-9 will help students understand the development of Greek civilization and its legacy for today.

Vocabulary Strategy: Use Word Origins
Activity Master, page 36

Have students use dictionaries to find the origin of the word *oracle*. Explain that the word comes from the Latin *orare* which means "to speak." Guide students to: define the word; explain how the definition is related to the word origin; and then check their definition against that in the notes.

Have students follow these steps as they complete the Activity Master.

Strategy Tip: Take Notes

Point out that taking notes can help students track and recall information. Students can turn article titles and subheads into questions, then read to answer the questions. For example:

Why did the Greeks visit Delphi?
Who were the great rivals?
What was life like in Athens? In Sparta?

My Notes

Down to the Sea in Ships
(pages 10–15)

Preview

Ask students to think of instances today in which geography plays an important role in the development of a nation or a culture. Call attention to the map on page 7 and ask:

How did the sea divide the Greeks?

How did the sea influence how ancient Greeks lived and worked?

Tell students to look for answers as they read.

Read Strategically: Recognize Cause-and-effect Relationships
Graphic Organizer, page 87

Have students use the graphic organizer as a reading guide. Ask them to look for facts relating to geographic features of Greece and the consequences of these features. Have them classify their findings into causes and effects.

Respond

Invite pairs of students to do research about the kinds of fish found in the Mediterranean Sea as well as different crops grown on rugged Greek farmland. Then, have each pair select one kind of fish (such as tuna) or crop (such as olive) and look up and copy a recipe using that food. Compile the recipes into a "From Ancient Times to Today" cookbook.

Going to the Games
(pages 16–21)

Preview

Ask who has watched the Olympic Games on TV. Briefly discuss some of the events and the athletes. Direct students to the vocabulary words on page 19: **hoplites**, **pentathlon** and **pankration**. Ask students to use context clues to describe these athletic events and to tell which ones are still Olympic events.

Read Strategically: Identify Main Ideas and Details

Remind students that one way to find main ideas in an article is to ask themselves what the article (or section of the article) is mainly about. Have students divide a sheet of paper into two columns—one labeled "Main Ideas" and the other labeled "Details." In the first column, ask students to write the main ideas in each section of the article. In the second column, opposite each main idea, students should list details that support and describe each of the main ideas.

Respond

Ask students to imagine that they are TV commentators, reporting on one event in the ancient Greek Olympic Games. Invite student commentators to write a set of notes they can use to describe the event. Then ask volunteers to report on events to the rest of the class.

A Visit to Delphi
(pages 22–25)

Preview

Invite students to share any myths they may know. Point out that myths are legendary stories, often about gods. Frequently, myths explain some natural phenomenon that humans aren't able to explain. Tell students that in this article they will read about a Greek myth.

Read Strategically: Sequence
Graphic Organizer, page 85

Tell students to fill in the flow chart to show the steps a pilgrim would follow on a visit to Delphi.

Respond

Brainstorm with the class to develop a list of natural phenomena that could not be easily explained in ancient Greece. Some examples might be a tidal wave, an eclipse, or a volcanic eruption. Have groups of students work together to create a myth explaining one of the phenomena listed. Remind students that the characters in the myth can be both Greek gods and mortals. When groups have finished writing, ask for volunteers to read their myths to the class.

The Great Rivals
(pages 26–31)

Preview

Have students briefly scan the article, noting the title, headings, illustrations and their captions, to get a sense of how the lifestyles in Athens and Sparta differed. Challenge students to make predictions about the article by asking:

In what ways do you think these two city-states differed from each other? What makes you think so?

Why might these differences lead to a great rivalry?

Read Strategically: Compare and Contrast
Activity Master, page 37

Have students use the Venn diagram to guide their reading. As they read, have them take notes about life in Athens, life in Sparta, and information common to both city-states.

Respond

Have students use their completed Activity Masters to discuss these questions:

How did the values of Athens and Sparta differ? (See pages 28-29.) **(compare and contrast)**

How did the education systems reflect what was important to each city-state? (See pages 28-29.) **(make judgments)**

Why did Athens and Sparta become military allies? (See page 31.) **(cause and effect)**

The Parthenon: Home for a Goddess (pages 32–35)

Preview

Ask students to name and describe some memorials or monuments in their own town or city. Discuss why these structures were built, and what the architects wanted visitors to think about when looking at the monuments. Tell students they will read an article about a very famous building in Athens.

Read Strategically: Draw Conclusions

Ask students to write the following questions on a sheet of paper, leaving space to record answers as they read.

What is the Parthenon?

What features give the Parthenon balance and harmony?

When they have finished, ask them to write a paragraph stating conclusions they have drawn about the classical style of architecture. Explain that drawing conclusions involves combining information you read with what you already know. If necessary, model how to draw conclusions.

Respond

Have students conduct library or Internet research on the Parthenon. On the basis of their research, have groups of students prepare a "Guide to the Parthenon."

The Power of the People (pages 36–41)

Preview

Prompt students to recall the meaning of *democracy* and its Greek origin. Then ask them to read the introduction on pages 36-37. Ask:

How do you think democracy in ancient Greece differed from democracy in the U.S. today?

Have students keep this question in mind as they read the article.

Read Strategically: Make Generalizations
Activity Master, page 38

Have students use the Activity Master as a study guide. As they read, they can write examples to support each generalization about democracy in ancient Greece. Then students can write a generalization of their own and provide examples to support it.

Respond

Organize the class into two teams to debate the issue: *Socrates was correct in choosing to die in obedience to Athenian law.* Have students set the rules for the debate (e.g., how many speakers, how long a speaker can talk) and ask team members to prepare notes for oral arguments. Provide time to hold the debate.

Problem Solvers
(pages 42–45)

Preview
Ask students to name the steps in the scientific method. Then ask them to imagine that there was no such thing as a scientific method. Explain that in this article students will explore how two ancient Greeks applied observation, mathematics and reasoning to solve problems, and in doing so, laid the basis for modern science.

Read Strategically: Summarize
Write these two statements on the board and have students copy them in their notebooks.

Hippocrates is called "the Father of Medicine."

Archimedes was both mathematician and inventor.

As students read the article, have them summarize in their own words information presented under each subhead.

Respond
Have students imagine they have been assigned to write an obituary for Archimedes or Hippocrates for a Greek newspaper. The obituary should include dates of birth and death, cause of death, accomplishments in life, and why he was an important person. Encourage students to use library and Internet resources for additional information.

In Search of Troy
(pages 46–51)

Preview
Use the photo and the text on pages 46–47 to start a discussion of the Trojan War. Elicit from students what they know about the legend of the Trojan horse and sources of this knowledge.

Read Strategically: Recognize Cause-and-effect Relationships
Graphic Organizer, page 87
Distribute copies of the graphic organizer. Ask students to list these causes on it:

A Trojan prince stole a Greek woman from her husband.

Frank Calvert believed Troy was buried at Hisarlik.

Schliemann found many ancient objects at Hisarlik.

Schliemann used clumsy digging methods.

As students read the article, have them fill in the effect (or effects) for each cause.

Respond
Have students work in groups to plan a "Meet the Archaeologist" TV program. One group member can role-play the part of Schliemann, Frank Calvert, or Manfred Korfmann. Other members of the group can prepare interview questions. Provide time for one or two volunteer groups to "produce" their program.

Alexander the Great
(pages 52–55)

Preview
Call attention to the title of this article and ask students what characteristics would make a person "great." Would these characteristics be exaggerated after the person died? Explain that in this article, students will read some of the stories that were told after the death of a man who was called Alexander the Great.

Read Strategically: Infer
Pose this question to the class:

What can you infer about Alexander's personality and characteristics from the legends that were told about him after his death?

Ask students to write this question in their notebooks. As they read the article, have them take notes that will help them answer it. Point out that inferring allows readers to "read between the lines" and use clues in the text to figure out what is not directly stated by the writer.

Respond
Have students use their notes to discuss: *(1) whether they think Alexander was really a world class hero* (**make judgments**); and *(2) what they think are the viewpoints of the people who created these legends.* (**identify point of view**)

Encourage students to justify their responses.

Focus on Skills

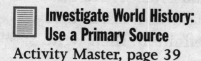 **Investigate World History: Use a Primary Source**

Activity Master, page 39

Explain that a primary source is a record provided by someone who actually saw the event. In most cases, primary sources record truthful observations. However, they can also be inaccurate. In the Activity Master, the recorder is Herodotus, considered today as the first real historian. The excerpt describes the customs of one of the conquered peoples who were part of the Persian Empire. Have students read the excerpt and then answer the questions.

Investigate World History: Mapping the World of Alexander the Great

As an independent project, have students create a map showing the conquests of Alexander the Great. They can draw a map of their own. The map should include a title, a legend, a compass, and if possible, a scale. Students can research Alexander's conquests in textbooks, historical atlases, as well as on the Internet.

Assessment Options

Questions

Use the following questions during individual conferences, or ask students to write the answers in their notebooks:

1 In what ways did geography shape the Greek civilization?

2 How were Athens and Sparta different?

3 What contributions did the Greeks make to architecture? To medicine? To mathematics?

4 Why are the findings of Heinrich Schliemann important in reconstructing the history of ancient Greece?

5 How did the Athenians practice democracy?

Assessment Activity

Ask each student to create a travel poster to advertise one of the major attractions in ancient Greece.

Posters should include:

✓ an illustration that clearly identifies a particular place in ancient Greece

✓ the historical significance of the place

✓ reasons people would be interested in visiting the location

Multiple-choice Test

Use the multiple-choice test on page 78.

Home-school Connection

With family members, students can look in magazines and reference books for pictures of buildings with some of the classical features described in the article on the Parthenon. Why do family members think that so many monuments and memorials are built in the classical Greek style? Students can share their pictures and ideas with the class.

Vocabulary: Use Word Origins

Many English words come from words in other languages. You can often figure out the meaning of an English word from the meaning of the original word. Listed below are some ancient Greek words. Read the original word and its definition. Then write the definition of the English word. Use the notes and a dictionary.

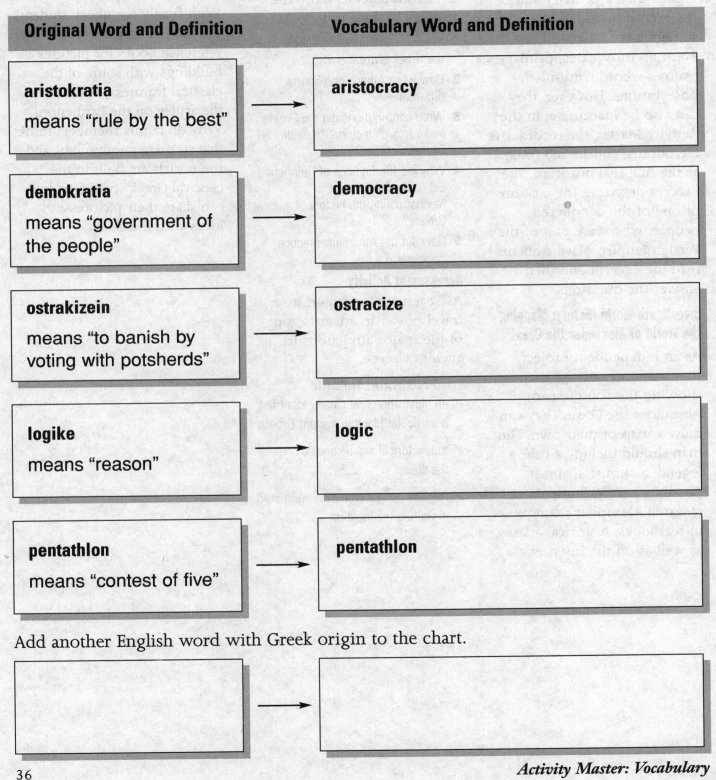

Original Word and Definition	Vocabulary Word and Definition
aristokratia means "rule by the best"	**aristocracy**
demokratia means "government of the people"	**democracy**
ostrakizein means "to banish by voting with potsherds"	**ostracize**
logike means "reason"	**logic**
pentathlon means "contest of five"	**pentathlon**

Add another English word with Greek origin to the chart.

Activity Master: Vocabulary

Read Strategically: Compare and Contrast

Use information from "The Great Rivals" to fill in the Venn diagram comparing Athens to Sparta. Include facts about lifestyles, values, education, entertainment and the arts, defense and the military. Write facts that apply to Athens on the left side and facts that apply to Sparta on the right. In the middle, write facts that apply to both. Then answer the question at the bottom of the page.

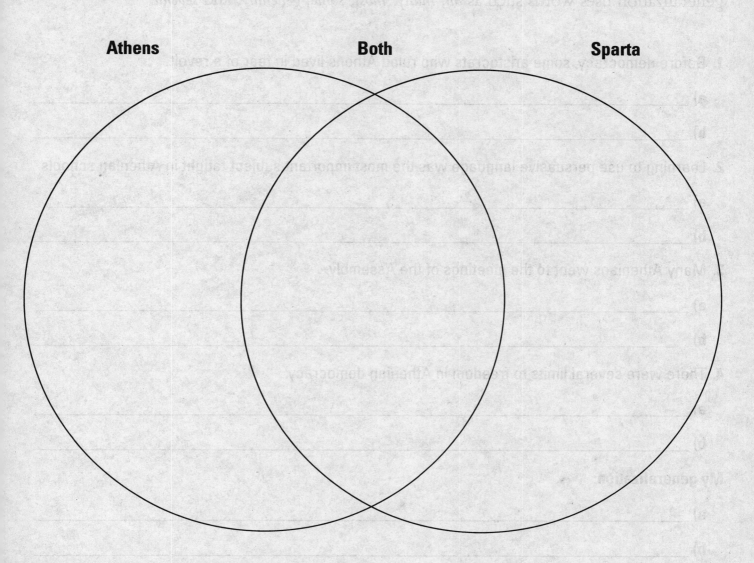

Athens   **Both**   **Sparta**

Why would Athens and Sparta become great rivals?

_____

_____

_____

Read Strategically: Make Generalizations

Below are four generalizations about democracy in ancient Greece. On the space beneath each generalization, write two examples that support it. Then write your own generalization about Greek democracy and provide two examples to support it.

Remember that a generalization is a kind of conclusion that applies to many examples. A generalization uses words such as *all, many, most, some, generally,* and *several.*

1. Before democracy, some aristocrats who ruled Athens lived in fear of a revolt.

   a) _____

   b) _____

2. Learning to use persuasive language was the most important subject taught in Athenian schools.

   a) _____

   b) _____

3. Many Athenians went to the meetings of the Assembly.

   a) _____

   b) _____

4. There were several limits to freedom in Athenian democracy.

   a) _____

   b) _____

My generalization:

   a) _____

   b) _____

Investigate World History: Use a Primary Source

The Greek Herodotus is thought to be the world's first historian. His books, *The Histories,* tell of the building of the Persian Empire. In the following excerpt—a primary source—he describes one of the customs of the conquered people of Thrace.

Use information from the excerpt below to answer the questions that follow.

Every five years, the Thracians choose one of their number by lot and send him to God as a messenger, with instructions to ask him for whatever they may happen to want; to effect the dispatch, some of them with javelins in the hands arrange themselves in a suitable position, while others take hold of the messenger by his hands and feet, and swing him up into the air in such a way as to make him fall upon the upturned points of the javelins.

(Herodotus, *The Histories,* Book 4, section 94)

1. Do you think that Herodotus actually saw this event take place? Why or why not?

_____

2. What details does Herodotus include that might be fact checked in other references?

_____

3. How do you think Herodotus feels about this custom? What makes you think so?

_____

4. What does the excerpt suggest about the customs of the Thracians?

_____

You want to learn more about the history of ancient Greece. Here are some sources you might read. Check the sources that are primary sources.

_____ A biography of Herodotus written in 1800

_____ Letters written by a Spartan soldier during the Peloponnesian War

_____ A chapter on the legacy of ancient Greece in a world history textbook

_____ A speech delivered by Pericles, an Athenian leader

_____ Excerpts from a medical book written by Hippocrates

_____ A website on Greek mythology

Ancient Rome
古罗马

"Ancient Rome" explores the growth of Rome from a small city-state into a far-reaching empire. The text is organized around three Big Ideas: The Rise of Rome; Challenges to the Empire; and The Legacy of Rome.

Summary

The Rise of Rome describes factors critical for empire building. Articles include: "Carthage Must Be Destroyed!"; "All Roads Lead to Rome"; and "Hail, Caesar!"

Challenges to the Empire explores problems arising from the spread of Christianity as well as from governing a widespread empire. This section includes: "Bread & Circuses"; "A New Faith"; and "Defending the Wall."

The Legacy of Rome discusses how the culture of ancient Rome influences our world today. Articles in this section are: "Time Capsule, A.D. 79"; "Rome Was Not Built in a Day"; and "The Glory of Rome."

Background

A large part of the story of Rome is one of empire building and political intrigue. Three factors contributed to the rise of Roman Empire: the army, a system of roads, and the rule of one powerful individual. At its height, the Roman Empire included large parts of Europe, Asia Minor and North Africa. This powerful empire left behind a legacy of government and law, language and literature, and architecture and public works. Over time, the Roman Empire weakened, was divided into eastern and western parts, and finally fell to invaders from the North in A.D. 476.

For additional historical background, see the Overview on pages 116-122.

Learning Objectives

Genre/Text Features

- expository
- article titles and subheads
- illustrations and photographs with captions
- maps, time lines and diagrams
- contents, overview and notes
- sidebars

Reading Skills

Skill Focus
- identify main ideas and details
- identify problems and solutions
- relate words

Supporting Skills
- use visuals to aid comprehension
- recognize cause-and-effect relationships
- draw conclusions

Writing/Communication Skills

Writing
- write a report
- write a compare/contrast paragraph
- write an essay

Speaking/Listening
- read aloud

Social Studies Skills

- trace routes on a map
- compare republican and authoritarian governments
- describe the importance of the system of Roman roads
- recognize some problems of an expanding empire
- cite examples of the Roman legacy
- analyze a time line

Focus on Content Area Reading

Before Reading

 ### Activate Prior Knowledge

Graphic Organizer, page 88

Refer students to the opening spread and text on pages 64-65. Ask:

What can you tell about ancient Rome from these pages?

Hand out copies of the KWL chart and have them write what they know about ancient Rome in the first column. Then ask students to read pages 66-69 and jot down what they would like to learn about this subject. Tell students to refer to their charts as they read. When they have finished, have them record in the third column major facts they have learned about ancient Rome.

Preview

Give students a few minutes to flip through "Ancient Rome" to see how it is organized.

Have them identify the various text features, such as the three Big Ideas, maps, time lines, introductory paragraphs, Why It Matters Today feature at the end of each article, and the Overview on pages 116-122. Guide students to recognize how exploring the three Big Ideas will give many insights into the history and legacy of ancient Rome.

Set Purpose

Help students to identify some practical reasons for studying ancient Rome. Ask:

Why is it important today to understand how a civilization developed, became powerful, and finally declined?

Vocabulary Strategy: Relate Words

Graphic Organizer, page 90

Distribute the concept web. Have students write *Roman Government* in the center circle, and each of the following words in one of the outside circles: *republic*; *Senate*; *dictator*; and *forum*.

Ask students to use the notes and a dictionary to write a definition for each word. Then have them write a sentence telling how the word relates to the Roman government. Students can create a second concept web for *Roman Army*, using the following words: *auxiliary*; *century*; *cohort*; and *legion*.

Strategy Tip: Use Visuals to Aid Comprehension

Encourage students to refer to the visuals and captions for information that helps explain or support text. Model how a reader might use the map on page 72 and the captioned illustration on page 73 to better understand military tactics described in the text.

My Notes

Focus on Content Area Reading (continued)

Carthage Must Be Destroyed! (pages 70–75)

Preview
Have students read the introductory paragraph on page 71 and look at the map on page 72 to discover where Carthage was located and predict why it had to be destroyed.

Read Strategically: Recognize Cause-and-effect Relationships
Graphic Organizer, page 87
Write the following topics on the board. Ask students to write at least one cause and its effect(s) related to each topic on the Activity Master.

- *the first Punic War*
- *the battle at Cannae*
- *the second Punic War*
- *the Roman army*
- *Roman building projects*

Respond
Invite volunteers to trace Hannibal's route from Spain to Cannae and Scipio's route from Rome to Zama on a wall map. Volunteers should point out Spain, France (Gaul), Italy, the Mediterranean Sea, Rhône River, the Alps and Appennines, Rome, Carthage and Sicily. Have students discuss the various hardships that both armies suffered following these routes.

All Roads Lead to Rome (pages 76–81)

Preview
Direct students to the chart on page 79 and discuss how the U. S. Interstate Highway system impacts modern-day life.

Read Strategically: Draw Conclusions
Write this question on the board and have students copy it in their notebooks:
How did the system of roads and bridges contribute to economic life and the defense of Rome?

As they read the article, have them take notes that will help them answer it. When students have finished reading, ask them to write conclusions they can draw about the impact of Roman roads on the expansion of the Roman Empire.

Respond
Initiate a classroom discussion on how Roman history might have been different if the Romans had not been such good builders of roads, bridges, aqueducts, walls and forts. Remind students to consider:

- *how the roads united the territory under Roman control;*
- *how the roads affected trade and travel; and*
- *how the road systems related to military security.*

Hail Caesar! (pages 82–85)

Preview
Point out that in the title of the article, the word *Caesar* refers to Julius Caesar, shown on page 82. However, alternative definitions also include "a tyrant or dictator" as well as "the title given to some Roman emperors." Ask students what they can tell about Julius Caesar from his statue and the information on page 83.

Read Strategically: Sequence
Graphic Organizer, page 86
Have students fill in events in the life of Julius Caesar as they read the article.

Respond
Initiate a class discussion to assess reading comprehension. Ask:

Why did Caesar defy the Senate's orders and decide to return to Rome? (See page 84.) **(make inferences)**

Why was Caesar killed and what was the long-term effect of his death? (See page 85.) **(cause and effect)**

Bread & Circuses
(pages 86–91)

Preview
Have students read the article title and the paragraph on page 87. Discuss the meaning of "bread and circuses," and ask students why a government might use such a technique.

Read Strategically: Identify Main Ideas and Details
Activity Master, page 46

Have students use the Activity Master as they read to help them identify the main ideas and details of the article.

Respond
Ask students to write a paragraph comparing and contrasting the gladiator combats in ancient Rome with an event such as the Superbowl, a playoff NBA game, or a hockey championship game. The paragraph should consider:

- *appearance of the stadium on game day;*
- *entrance of the teams;*
- *the game and its outcome; and*
- *reactions of the fans.*

Provide time for students to read their paragraphs aloud to the class.

A New Faith
(pages 92–95)

Preview
Write the terms *tolerant* and *persecution* on the board. Ask students to define these terms and use each in a sentence that relates to our world today. Have students read the opening paragraph on page 93 and ask:

> *Why might the Romans consider people who worshiped their own God dangerous to Roman society?*

Tell students that in this article they will find out how the new faith of Christianity affected the history of the Roman Empire.

Read Strategically: Recognize Cause-and-effect Relationships
Graphic Organizer, page 87

On the graphic organizer, have students fill in five cause-and-effect relationships described in the article.

Respond
Initiate a discussion to assess reading comprehension. Ask:

> *In what ways were Christians persecuted?* (See page 95.) **(main ideas and details)**

> *Despite persecutions, why did Christianity continue to spread?* (See page 95.) **(draw conclusions)**

> *Why do you think the Roman government changed its policy toward Christians?* **(make judgments)**

Defending the Wall
(pages 96–99)

Preview
Remind students that the Roman Empire extended into three continents: Europe, Africa and Asia. Discuss with students some problems that might arise from having to control such a widespread territory. Ask what the Romans might do to protect their lands.

Read Strategically: Identify Problems and Solutions
Activity Master, page 47

Have students use the Activity Master as a reading guide. Have them fill in solutions for each of the five problems resulting from an expanding empire.

Respond
Invite students to use the description of building the wall to draw a diagram showing the wall's features. (You can encourage interested students to make a model.) When everyone has finished, ask volunteers to share and explain their diagrams with the class.

Time Capsule A.D. 79
(pages 100-105)

Preview

Have students thumb through the article, noting especially the visuals and their captions. Ask:

> *Why do you think this article is called "Time Capsule"?*

> *What happened in Pompeii in A.D. 79?*

Have students read the article to see if their responses were accurate.

Read Strategically: Summarize

Graphic Organizer, page 90

Have students use the concept web to classify various aspects of life in ancient Pompeii. They can write *Life in Ancient Pompeii* in the center circle and *Street Life, Cooking and Eating, Shops,* and *Leisure and Entertainment* on the four outer circles.

Respond

Have students use library or Internet resources to write an eyewitness account describing the eruption of Mount Vesuvius for a nightly TV news program. Remind students that the news report should try to answer the questions: *Who? What? Where? When?* and *Why?*

Rome Was Not Built in a Day (pages 106-111)

Preview

Ask students to skim through this article, noting especially the visuals. Then write these questions on the board:

> *What do you predict this article will be about?*

> *Why wasn't Rome built in a day?*

Then have students read to verify, modify or change their predictions.

Read Strategically: Draw Conclusions

Pose this question to the class:

> *How did the Romans build buildings and aqueducts that lasted such a long time?*

As they read the article, have them take notes that will help them answer it. When they have finished reading, ask them to cite conclusions they can draw about the Romans as engineers and builders.

Respond

Challenge students to use library and Internet resources to write a brief essay on the features of Roman architecture.

An excellent starting place is http://www.2020site.org/rome.

Suggest students illustrate their essays with photos of American buildings that reflect the features of Roman buildings.

The Glory of Rome
(pages 112-115)

Preview

Ask students to imagine that the year is now 3005. What do they think will be the legacy of China? What features of Chinese culture—architecture, government and laws, language and literature, and customs—might remain? Do students think they might pick up a book and find a chapter entitled "The Glory of China"?

Read Strategically: Make Connections

Have students write the six subheads in the article in their notebooks. As they read, tell them to list at least one legacy under each subhead. When they have finished, ask them to write what they found most interesting about the link between the culture of ancient Rome and their lives today.

Respond

Initiate a class discussion to assess reading comprehension. Ask:

> *What are some practices or features in U.S. government and laws that come from ancient Rome?* (See pages 53-54.) **(main ideas and details)**

> *What do you think is Rome's most important legacy, and why?* (See pages 113-115.) **(make judgments)**

Focus on Skills

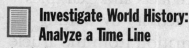

Investigate World History: Analyze a Time Line
Activity Master, page 48

Have students use information on the time line to complete the Activity Master. When students have finished, they can exchange papers with a partner and discuss answers.

Writing and Research: Write a Report
Activity Master, page 49

Have students choose one Roman ruler they have read about in the book and write a report about that man's life and accomplishments. Students can research and include additional information from reference books or the Internet. Have them organize their information on the Activity Master before they write their report.

Assessment Options

Questions
Use the following questions during individual conferences, or ask students to write the answers in their notebooks:

1 Why were the Romans determined to conquer Carthage?

2 How did the system of roads, bridges and aqueducts benefit the Romans?

3 Why did Rome change from a republic to an empire?

4 Why was the Christian religion a threat to the Romans?

5 What are least three examples of Rome's legacy to today's world? Explain your answer.

Assessment Activity
Have students use pictures and captions to represent the Big Ideas highlighted on page 69 of this book. Students can cut pictures from magazines, create their own illustrations, or print visuals from the Internet. They will need to write a caption for each picture. The visual representation should:

✓ address all three Big Ideas

✓ include images that relate to the Big Ideas

✓ use captions that clearly explain picture selections

✓ state how each image relates to one of the Big Ideas

✓ be well-organized and carefully prepared

Multiple-choice Test
Use the multiple-choice test on page 79.

Home-school Connection

Students and family members can use the information on page 114 to begin to compile a list of words that have a basis in Latin (such as *legal* from the Latin *legalis*) or are Latin terms (such as *alumnus/alumna*). Students can share their lists with the class. To extend the activity, invite interested volunteers to compile the lists into a dictionary.

Ancient Rome

Read Strategically: Identify Main Ideas and Details

The main ideas of an article are what it is mostly about. Details are facts and examples that support and explain each main idea. Complete the following activity by writing two or more details that support the main ideas stated. Use information from the article "Bread & Circuses."

1. Main Idea: Gladiators used different kinds of weapons, armor and fighting styles.

   Details: _____

   _____

   _____

2. Main Idea: The Colosseum was built for combat between men and animals.

   Details: _____

   _____

   _____

3. Main Idea: Some emperors were great fans of combat at the Colosseum.

   Details: _____

   _____

   _____

4. Main Idea: A typical day at the Colosseum was a bloody spectacle.

   Details: _____

   _____

   _____

5. Main Idea: There were several reasons for the end of the gladiator combats.

   Details: _____

   _____

   _____

Read Strategically: Identify Problems and Solutions

As you read "Defending the Wall," think about the problems the Romans faced as they tried to expand and control their empire. Describe how the Romans tried to solve each problem listed.

Problem	Solution
1. Sending additional troops from Rome to distant provinces was a money-losing proposition.	
2. Soldiers recruited from conquered lands needed some incentive or reason to fight for Rome.	
3. The Romans had been unsuccessful in conquering invading tribes who lived farther north in Britannia.	
4. In building Hadrian's Wall, the Romans had to plan a way for Roman soldiers to search the landscape from coast to coast for trouble.	
5. As the wall was built, the Romans had to plan a system for keeping the news traveling quickly from one point to another.	

Investigate World History: Analyze a Time Line

A time line shows when events took place in the past. Use information from the time line below to complete this activity.

Major Events: Ancient Rome

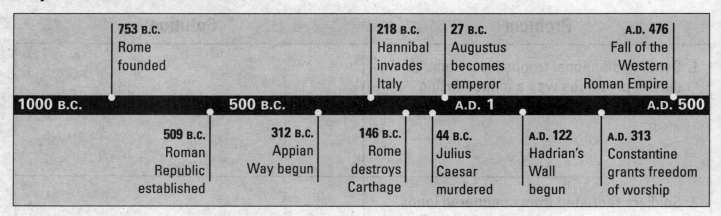

1. How many years are covered on this time line?

   _____

2. How many years passed between the founding of Rome and the fall of the Western Roman Empire?

   _____

3. Which two events shown on the time line relate to the Punic Wars?

   _____

4. In what year did Emperor Constantine grant Christians and non-Christians the freedom to worship the religion they chose?

   _____

5. Which came first, the beginning of work on the Appian Way or the beginning of work on Hadrian's Wall?

   _____

6. What event occurred in 27 B.C.? Why is this event important?

   _____

Write a Report

You will be writing a report on one ruler you read about in "Ancient Rome." Whom will you choose? Organize your ideas on this activity sheet before you write. Then write your report on another sheet of paper.

Ruler's name: _____

Dates when he ruled: _____

I. How he came to power

A. _____

B. _____

II. What problems he faced, or what he wanted to do

A. _____

B. _____

III. How he solved his problems or achieved his goals

A. _____

B. _____

IV. Why he was an important ruler

A. _____

B. _____

Other information to include _____

_____

_____

My sources: _____

_____

_____

From the Middle Ages to Renaissance
从中世纪到文艺复兴

The Middle Ages 中世纪

"The Middle Ages" book explores events, people, and institutions that influenced life during the Middle Ages. The text looks at three Big Ideas: Power of the Church; Growth of Cities and Towns; and the Legacy of the Middle Ages.

Summary

Power of the Church

examines some of the ways in which the Church influenced medieval life, from architecture to the Crusades. Articles include: "Towers of Faith and Stone"; "A Monk's Life"; and "Holy War, A.D. 1099."

Growth of Cities and Towns

traces the development and effects of growing urbanization, increased trade, and a new type of economy. Articles in this section include: "City at the Crossroads: Constantinople"; "A Busy World"; and "The Black Death."

Legacy of the Middle Ages

describes changes in government, scientific thinking, and warfare that were to influence modern life. In this section are: "King John & Magna Carta"; "The Philosopher's Stone"; and "Arrows vs. Armor."

Background

The term *Middle Ages* describes the period between the fall of Rome in 476 and the end of the Hundred Years War in 1453. It is the historic period that falls in the middle—between the ancient world and the Renaissance. It was a time of faith, constant war and daily hardships. Yet it was also a time of advances in the economy, government, and the arts and sciences.

The Overview on pages 56-62 provides a useful summary of some of the political and social highlights as well as important changes that occurred during these tumultuous years.

Learning Objectives

Genre/Text Features

- expository
- article titles and subheads
- sidebars
- contents, overview and notes
- illustrations and photographs with captions
- maps, time lines and diagrams

Reading Skills

Skill Focus
- recognize cause-and-effect relationships
- identify main ideas and details
- relate words

Supporting Skills
- compare and contrast
- sequence
- summarize

Writing/Communicaton Skills

Writing
- write "A Day in the Life of a Medieval…" article
- write a descriptive paragraph
- create a page for an illuminated manuscipt

Speaking/Listening
- give an oral presentation
- have a panel discusssion

Social Studies Skills

- examine the role of the Church during the Middle Ages
- recognize importance of a city's location to trade
- describe work and life in a medieval town
- recognize the political importance of the Magna Carta
- explain why the Battle of Crécy was a turning point

Before Reading

Activate Prior Knowledge

Refer students to the photograph on pages 4-5 and have them read the title and caption. Begin a concept web on the board and write *Middle Ages* in the center. Ask students how they imagine life during this historical period. Record their responses on the web. Then have students read pages 6-9 and add other images and ideas about medieval life. Point out that the three Big Ideas they will explore in "The Middle Ages" highlight significant features of medieval life.

Preview

Give students a few minutes to look over the table of contents and to flip through "The Middle Ages" to see how it is organized. Point out text features such as Why It Matters Today and the Overview.

Ask:

How is "The Middle Ages" organized?

What is the Overview? How might you use this feature?

Will you be reading about the past, the present, or both?

Set Purpose

Discuss why it is important to know what happened during the Middle Ages. Note that some of the changes that occurred during this time helped to shape our lives today. Tell students that they will find links from the past to the present in the Why It Matters Today feature at the end of each article.

Vocabulary Strategy: Relate Words

Activity Master, page 56

Write the words *feudal,* and *chivalry* on the board. Ask students to look up the meaning of each word in the dictionary and tell how the word relates to the Middle Ages. Then assign students to complete the Activity Master.

Strategy Tip: Ask Questions

If students have difficulty understanding parts of an article, suggest they turn the Big Ideas, article titles, and subheads into questions and then read to answer the questions. For example:

What powers did the Church have?

What are towers of faith and stone?

My Notes

Towers of Faith and Stone
(pages 10–15)

Preview
Ask students to read the introductory paragraph on page 11 and then study the photograph of the Chartres Cathedral on page 12. Ask how this picture shows the importance of the church. Use the picture to reinforce the idea that the Church dominated many aspects of life during the Middle Ages.

Read Strategically: Sequence
Graphic Organizer, page 85

Have students use the flow chart to guide their reading of this article. Guide them to note the stages of the process that workers followed in building a cathedral.

Respond
Ask students to imagine they are workers helping to build the cathedral at Beauvais. Have them write a descriptive paragraph of the scene that might have occurred when the cathedral collapsed. Urge them to use cathedral-related words such as *buttress*, *piers*, and *stained glass windows*. You might want students to include illustrations to accompany their descriptions. Call on volunteers to read their descriptions aloud.

A Monk's Life
(pages 16–21)

Preview
Refer students to the title, introductory text and photographs on pages 16 and 19 and ask what these features tell about a monk's life. Help students relate the words *monk* and *monastery* to each other. Then invite students to predict what other information they might read about in this article.

Read Strategically: Identify Details
Graphic Organizer, page 90

Have students fill in the concept web as they read the article. Tell them to write *A Monk's Life* in the center circle and then record details about the topic (rules, different jobs, prayers) in the outer circles.

Respond
Have students use their notes to discuss these questions:

What were the characteristics of a monk's life during the Middle Ages? (See pages 16-21.) **(summarize)**

Why do you think monks chose this way of life? **(make judgments)**

How did monks contribute to the power of the Church? **(infer)**

Holy War A.D. 1099
(pages 22–25)

Preview
Have students read the introductory paragraph on page 22 and locate Palestine and Jerusalem on the map on page 25. Ask them to predict why Jerusalem was so important to both Christians and Muslims. Point out that the Near East referred to a region that included the countries of southwest Asia from the Mediterranean Sea to Iran, plus part of northeastern Africa. Today, the region is usually called the Middle East.

Read Strategically: Visualize
Encourage students to use the images in the article to help them visualize the geography (climate and landscape) of the holy war, the contrast between the Crusaders and the Muslim defenders, and the final attack on Jerusalem. Remind students to use the images to help them define unfamiliar vocabulary such as *jihad*, *siege*, and *catapults*.

Respond
Initiate a class discussion to assess comprehension. Ask:

In what ways were the Muslim defenders and the Christian attackers alike? In what ways were they different? (See page 24.) **(compare and contrast)**

Why was the conquest of Jerusalem important to the Church? (See pages 22-24.) **(draw conclusions)**

City at the Crossroads: Constantinople (pages 26–29)

Preview

Have students read the title on page 26 and study the map on page 28. Discuss the meaning of the word *crossroads*. Then ask how the map shows that Constantinople is a crossroads city and how its location might affect the lives of the people living there.

Read Strategically: Recognize Cause-and-effect Relationships
Graphic Organizer, page 87

Write the following topics on the board and ask students to write at least one cause and its effect(s) related to each topic on the graphic organizer:

- *location along major land trade routes*
- *location along major water trade routes*
- *lifestyles of the wealthy*
- *producing silk*
- *consequences of wealth*

Respond

Ask students to imagine that they are reporters for a business magazine. Have them work with a partner to write an interview with a wealthy merchant at his stall on the Mese. The interview should include questions and answers about the merchant's work, as well as his lifestyle. If time permits, have student pairs role-play their interviews.

A Busy World (pages 30–35)

Preview

Ask students to explain what an *economy* is. Guide them to recognize that an economy is generally any activity that relates to producing, distributing, and consuming goods and services. Invite students to predict some of the characteristics of the economy of a medieval town and then read the article to verify their predictions.

Read Strategically: Make Judgments
Graphic Organizer, page 88

Have students use the KWL chart as a reading guide. Before reading, have them fill in what they already know about work and life in a medieval town and what they want to learn. As they read, ask them to fill in facts they have learned. Then discuss what they found most interesting about life in a medieval town.

Respond

To assess comprehension, ask:

Why did people spend so much time in the market square? (See pages 32-33.) **(draw conclusions)**

What kind of work might a peasant find in a medieval town? (See pages 33 and 35.) **(summarize)**

How does life in a medieval town compare with life in your community today? **(compare and contrast)**

The Black Death (pages 36–41)

Preview

Explain that an epidemic is a disease that affects a huge number of people at the same time. Challenge students to name some epidemics that have taken place within their lifetime. Tell students that this article is about a terrible epidemic that occurred during the Middle Ages.

Read Strategically: Recognize Cause-and-effect Relationships
Activity Master, page 57

Have students read the article independently and identify at least one cause-and-effect relationship. Remind them that the effect is what happens and the cause is why it happens. Encourage them to add other causes and effects they find to the Activity Master.

Respond

Call on volunteers to assume the role of experts on a panel discussing the causes and spread of the Black Death. The panel can consist of an astrologer, priest, doctor, and a historian. Have the rest of the class assume the role of reporters asking panel members questions.

King John & Magna Carta
(pages 42–47)

Preview

Ask: *What is the purpose of the Constitution?* Help students understand that it is a plan of government as well as a document that protects people's basic rights and establishes a rule of law for all. Explain that in this article students will learn that some of the ideas reflected in the Constitution of the United States have their roots in the Middle Ages.

Read Strategically: Sequence
Graphic Organizer, page 85

Have students use the flow chart to guide their reading of the article. Ask them to fill in the major events that led to King John's signing of the Magna Carta.

Respond

Invite students to write a news story about the Magna Carta and the events leading up to its signing. Remind them to answer the five questions for a news story: *Who? What? When? Where?* and *Why?* and to write a headline for their article.

The Philosopher's Stone
(pages 48–51)

Preview

Tell students to imagine that they want to find out why some substances dissolve in water and others do not. Urge them to think about the steps involved in solving this problem. Note that these steps—observing, experimenting and drawing conclusions—are part of the scientific method. Explain that in this article students will read about the beginnings of the scientific method.

Read Strategically: Summarize

Ask students to write this question in their notebooks:

> *How did Roger Bacon contribute to scientific knowledge?*

Have students list facts that answer this question and use the facts to write a summary paragraph. Encourage students to rewrite the question as a topic sentence for their paragraph.

Respond

Ask students to imagine that they are filmmakers and want to make a TV movie called "The Philosopher's Stone." Call on volunteers to explain to a TV executive what their movie is about and why the network should produce it.

Arrows vs. Armor
(pages 52–55)

Preview

Have students read the title of this article and turn it into a question. Explain that the article not only describes how warfare changed during the Middle Ages, but also how this change challenged medieval values.

Reading Strategy: Identify Main Ideas and Details
Activity Master, page 58

Assign the article for independent reading. Have students use the Activity Master as a reading guide to help them identify main ideas and supporting details as they read. Explain that a reading selection may have one or more main ideas.

Respond

Initiate a class discussion to assess reading comprehension. Ask:

> *Why was the battle of Crécy an important turning point during the Middle Ages?* (See pages 54–55.) **(summarize)**

Focus on Skills

Map Activity: Compare and Contrast

Display a wall map of Europe or a world atlas. Have students use the references to locate the countries of Europe and major bodies of water. Then ask students to compare a map of Europe today with the map of medieval Europe on page 7.

Investigate World History: Create an Illuminated Manuscript

Have students refer to the photograph of the Book of Kells (page 20) or research other examples of illuminated manuscripts. Then invite them to work in small groups to create their own illuminated manuscript (art and text) for one or more pages of a book called "The Middle Ages." Each group can share its manuscript with the class. Students presenting the manuscript should:

✓ clearly state the main idea and details of the illumination

✓ relate the illumination to the text

✓ make eye contact with listeners

Listeners should:

✓ listen politely and not interrupt

✓ ask questions for clarification

Writing and Research: Life in Medieval Europe
Activity Master, page 59

Have students write about life in medieval times from the perspective of someone who actually lived during that time. First, have them choose a medieval person of interest to them, i.e., a Crusader, a monk, a peasant, a trader, or a craftsperson. Tell them to use the Activity Master to organize their writing. Encourage students to do additional research. Students can write a first-person narrative or an informational/expository report.

Assessment Options

Questions

Use the following questions during individual conferences, or ask students to write the answers in their notebooks:

1 In what ways did the Christian Church dominate many aspects of medieval life? Give examples to support your answer.

2 What problems did the Crusaders have to overcome before and during the battle to capture Jerusalem?

3 Why did Constantinople become the richest city in the medieval world? What were some effects of its wealth?

4 Would you have liked to live in a medieval town? Why or why not?

5 What was the purpose of the Magna Carta?

6 What factors helped to put an end to the "age of knighthood"?

Assessment Activity

Have students list or illustrate six or more items from the Middle Ages that they would put in a time capsule. Each item should:

✓ have a title

✓ include text that explains what it is or how it is used

✓ include text that gives reasons why it should be in the time capsule

Multiple-choice Test

Use the multiple-choice test on page 80.

Home-school Connection

With family members, students can look in newspapers and magazines for articles about epidemics in the world today. They can discuss why the Black Death killed so many people during medieval times and what is being done to prevent the spread of epidemics today.

Vocabulary: Relate Words

The words below are from "The Middle Ages." Each term has something to do with the people or events during that time. Use the notes in your student book to check your understanding of each word. Then write a sentence that shows how you think the word relates to the Middle Ages.

Word	Meaning	Sentence
alchemist		
cathedral		
chivalry		
guild		
medieval		
monastery		
plague		
pope		

Activity Master: Vocabulary

Read Strategically: Recognize Cause-and-effect Relationships

As you read "The Black Death," think about things that happened and why those things happened. To find the effects for each cause listed below, read the cause and ask yourself, "What happened as a result of this?" Remember, a cause may have more than one effect.

Cause: Why did it happen?	Effect: What happened?
1. Merchant ships stopped at cities in Asia, Africa and Europe to trade.	
2. Workers, from farmers to craftspeople, became scarce.	
3. Cities stopped trading with each other.	
4. Many people lost faith in the Church.	
5. People tried many remedies to cure the disease.	

Write a cause-and-effect statement relating to global epidemics today. Use the back of this paper.

Read Strategically: Identify Main Ideas and Details

The main ideas in the article "Arrows vs. Armor" tell what the article is mostly about. Details are facts and examples that explain and support the main ideas. Finish the activity below with details that support the main ideas in this article. Then choose a main idea of your own, write it in, and supply details about it.

1. **Main Idea:** *The battle at Crécy marked a turning point in warfare.*

   Details:

   - _____

   - _____

   - _____

2. **Main Idea:** *The new type of warfare signaled the beginning of the end of chivalry.*

   Details:

   - _____

   - _____

   - _____

3. **My Main Idea:**

   Details:

   - _____

   - _____

   - _____

Activity Master: Read Strategically

Write an Article

Imagine that you have been asked to write an article for a book about life during the Middle Ages. The book, called *A Day in the Life of...* is a collection of articles written by different people who actually lived at that time. Choose a person you have read about in "The Middle Ages" and describe a day in that person's life. For example, you could write about your life as a knight, an alchemist, a monk, or a peasant. You'll need to include details that are historically accurate as well as interesting to you. So, you might want to gather information from other resources in addition to what you read in this book.

Answer the questions below to help you organize your ideas before writing.

1. Who are you? Where do you live?

_____

2. Whom do you work for?

_____

3. What kind of work do you do?

_____

4. What do you like most about what you do? What do you like the least?

_____

5. How do you spend any free time you have?

_____

_____

Other things to write about:

_____

_____

_____

Now write your article on a separate piece of paper.

Renaissance 文艺复兴

"Renaissance" describes the extraordinary flowering of arts and sciences that marked the Renaissance. It also explores the Reformation and the development of new Christian churches.

The articles are organized around three Big Ideas: Birthplace of the Renaissance; Revolution in Art and Science; and Changing the Church.

Summary

Birthplace of the Renaissance examines the beginning of the Renaissance in the city-states of Italy. Articles include: "Power Struggle in Florence" and "The Glory of Venice."

Revolution in Art and Science describes how Renaissance painters revolutionized European art and Renaissance scientists discovered new ways of viewing the world. Articles include: "New Styles in Art"; "Da Vinci, the Renaissance Man"; and "A New Universe."

Changing the Church examines how the invention of the printing press and the publication of the Bible led to the development of new Protestant faiths throughout Europe as well as a reform movement in the Catholic Church. Articles include: "The Book That Changed the World"; "Here I Stand"; and "Elizabeth Learns to Rule."

Background

The Renaissance began in the 1300s in the wealthy and powerful city-states of Italy, where ideas of humanism, rediscovery of classical civilization, and realism led to a revolution in the arts, science and literature. This cultural "rebirth" soon spread to northern Europe. The bold spirit of the Renaissance launched still another period of history, the Age of Exploration.

In the 1440s, Gutenberg invented a printing press, which opened the door to a flood of books, spreading the ideas of humanists, scientists, and religious reformers, most notably Martin Luther. A new movement, the Reformation, arose, challenging many practices of the Catholic Church. Effects of the Reformation included religious wars, the creation of different Protestant churches, and reform in the Catholic Church.

Learning Objectives

Genre/Text Features

- expository
- article titles and subheads
- contents, overview and notes
- illustrations, photographs and captions
- maps, time lines and diagrams
- sidebars and features

Reading Skills

Skill Focus
- identify problems and solutions
- recognize cause-and-effect relationships
- relate words

Supporting Skills
- identify main ideas and details
- summarize
- sequence
- generalize

Writing/Communication Skills

Writing
- write a profile/biography
- create a travel brochure
- review a work of art

Speaking/Listening
- deliver a speech
- broadcast a news report

Social Studies Skills

- explain why the Renaissance began in the Italian city-states
- compare Renaissance and pre-Renaissance artistic styles
- name some Renaissance scientists and explain their ideas
- relate Martin Luther to the Reformation
- interpret a primary source

Focus on Content Area Reading

Before Reading

Activate Prior Knowledge

Invite students to share what they know about each period of history—where it started, what its characteristics were, what famous people lived during this time. Draw two webs on the board with *Renaissance* and *Reformation* written in the centers and students' responses radiating from it. Students can copy the webs in their notebooks. Then, when they read along, they can add key ideas and phrases to their webs.

Preview

Give students a few minutes to thumb through "Renaissance." Tell them to note its many features: the Big Ideas, Why It Matters Today, captioned images, and the Overview. Ask:

> *How is "Renaissance" organized?*

> *How might the Overview and other text features help you during the reading?*

Set Purpose

Have students choose a photograph in "Renaissance" that shows a way of life very different from their own. Invite them to discuss what living in such a place and time might have been like. Ask:

> *What do we gain from studying the way people lived in the past?*

Use this discussion to help students recognize that the way we live today owes much to the people and events of the past.

Vocabulary Strategy: Relate Words
Activity Master, page 66

Distribute the Activity Master and have students complete it using words relating to the Renaissance. Then, ask students to copy the graphic organizer (or distribute a second copy of the Master) and complete a similar activity relating the following words to the Reformation: *heretic*; *indulgence*; *movable type*; *pope*; and *Protestant*.

Strategy Tip: Use Images to Aid Comprehension

Remind students that captioned visuals provide information that aids reading comprehension. Students can ask questions as they examine the many visuals in each article, for example: What part of the text does this explain? What details does the caption provide about the subject of the visual? How the visual and its caption support the main ideas presented in the text? Tell students to reread to see how an image or a diagram best fits the text. If they have having difficulty, students can ask for clarification during a follow-up class discussion.

My Notes

Power Struggle in Florence
(pages 70–73)

Preview

Have students skim through this article, noting the title, images and their captions, and subheads. Ask them to predict the reason for the power struggle and who might have been involved.

Read Strategically: Recognize Cause-and-effect Relationships
Graphic Organizer, page 87

Have students use the cause-and-effect organizer to guide their reading. Under Cause(s), have them fill in the following: (1) *Because the Medicis were important patrons of the arts;* (2) *Because being wealthy also meant having great political power;* (3) *Because the Medicis prevented the Pazzis from gaining more political power;* and (4) *Because Lorenzo de Medici escaped from the Pazzi plot.* As students read the article, have them fill in the Effect(s) boxes and add one cause-and-effect statement of their own.

Respond

Have students work in small groups to write and produce a special segment for the evening news on the attack on the Medicis in the cathedral earlier in the day. The report should include a description of the events, reasons for the attack, and a profile of the Medici family. Provide time for groups to "broadcast" their reports.

The Glory of Venice
(pages 74–79)

Preview

Have students locate Venice on a wall map or on the map on page 67 and identify the body of water that borders the city. Ask students to use the map to explain why Venice became a wealthy center of trade.

Read Strategically: Make Generalizations

Review with students that a generalization is a type of conclusion that applies to many examples. Ask them to write these two generalizations in their notebooks and jot down examples that support each generalization as they read.

Venice was wed to the sea.

Venice was different from most other cities.

Respond

Have students work with a partner or in small groups to create a travel brochure for a tour of Venice, past to present. Encourage them to use pictures and vivid, descriptive language in their brochures. Suggest that students use the text, Internet, and other resources for their research.

New Styles in Art
(pages 80–85)

Preview

Bring to class and display some reproductions of medieval art. Ask students to compare the art displayed with the images on pages 80-81. Ask:

Which paintings are more lifelike?

In what other ways are the pictures in the book different from those displayed?

Read Strategically: Identify Problems and Solutions
Activity Master, page 67

Have students use the Activity Master to identify challenges that Renaissance painters faced as they set about to change the direction of European art. As students read the article, ask them to note the solutions to these problems.

Respond

Tell students to assume the role of art critic and analyze one of the paintings shown in the article. Their review should include: the painting's title; what the artist was trying to do; artistic techniques he used to achieve this goal; details that make the painting unique or revolutionary for the times; and the critic's own opinion.

Da Vinci, the Renaissance Man (pages 86-93)

Preview

Have students study the visuals in the article and read the opening paragraph on page 86. Ask:

What makes a person a "Renaissance Man"?

Challenge students to name other people who might be called "Renaissance Men or Women."

Read Strategically: Summarize

Tell students to jot down the many activities and accomplishments of Leonardo as they read. When they have finished, have them use their notes to write a summary paragraph based on this topic sentence: *Leonardo was truly a "Renaissance Man."*

Respond

Initiate a discussion to assess reading comprehension. Ask:

As a young man, how did Leonardo express his creativity? (See pages 88-89.) **(main ideas and details)**

Why did Leonardo choose to invent weapons at the same time he worked as a painter? (See page 90.) **(cause and effect)**

In what ways has Leonardo da Vinci influenced the modern world? (See pages 92–93.) **(draw conclusions)**

A New Universe (pages 94-99)

Preview

Have students read the introductory paragraph on page 95. Challenge students to identify ideas and discoveries that have changed the way people live, communicate and look at the world.

Read Strategically: Compare and Contrast

List the names of the four scientists profiled in this article on the board. Tell students as they read to note each scientist's new theory or discovery as well as the ancient idea it disproved.

Respond

Have students write a profile of one of the scientists mentioned in this article for a website. The entry should include date and place of the scientist's birth, his scientific contributions, and the significance of his work for future scientists. Encourage students to do additional research online or in print resources.

The Book That Changed the World (pages 100-103)

Preview

Have students read the article title and the opening paragraph, and examine the picture. Ask them to generate some questions they think the article might answer. Write these questions on the board. Encourage students to keep these questions in mind as they read the article.

Read Strategically: Recognize Cause-and-effect Relationships
Activity Master, page 68

Have students use the questions on the Activity Master to relate effects to causes as they read the article. Remind students that a cause is a reason that something happens and an effect is what happens.

Respond

Initiate a class discussion to assess reading comprehension. Ask:

What order of steps did Gutenberg follow to print on his new press? (See page 102.) **(sequence)**

In what ways was the Gutenberg Bible unique? (See pages 102-103.) **(main ideas and details)**

Why is this article titled "The Book That Changed the World"? (See page 103.) **(draw conclusions)**

"Here I Stand"
(pages 104–109)

Preview

Direct students to the image and its caption on pages 104-105. Call on a volunteer to describe the scene and people depicted. Ask if anyone knows the significance of the quote "Here I Stand" and who said it.

Read Strategically: Make Connections

Write this question on the board:

How did the ideas of reform (as in Reformation) and protest (as in Protestant) apply to Martin Luther's work and its effects?

Tell students to keep this question in mind as they read the article and jot down notes to answer it.

Respond

Initiate a discussion to assess reading comprehension. Ask:

Why did Luther protest the selling of indulgences? (See page 106.) **(cause and effect)**

Why was the printing press critical to the Reformation? (See page 107.) **(draw conclusions)**

Why do you think Luther's simple protest sparked a Reformation? (See page 108.)
(make judgments)

Elizabeth Learns to Rule
(pages 110–115)

Preview

Point out to the class that religion is often the source of many conflicts. For example, the Crusades were a series of wars between Christian Europeans and Muslims to capture Palestine from its Muslim rulers. Have students identify other instances where religion was/is a cause of conflict. Point out that students are going to read how Queen Elizabeth I handled religious conflict in England.

Read Strategically: Sequence Events
Graphic Organizer, page 86

Distribute copies of the time line chart. As students read the article, have them fill in facts and dates about the English rulers mentioned. Students will need to do some additional research to find dates for these events:

Mary I becomes queen.

Sir Thomas More is beheaded.

Anne Boleyn is executed.

Students can add these dates and events to their time lines.

Respond

Invite students to work with a partner and imagine they are Queen Elizabeth's speech writers. They must write a speech Elizabeth will give after she is crowned queen of England. The speech should include facts about Elizabeth's childhood, how she came to be queen, and her hopes for England. Students should use facts from this article as well as from other sources.

Provide time for students to deliver their speeches.

Focus on Skills

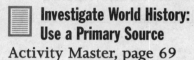 **Investigate World History: Use a Primary Source**

Activity Master, page 69

Explain that we learn about the past through either primary or secondary sources. Primary sources are records left by people who actually witnessed an event. Primary sources may be in the form of written records, artifacts, paintings, film, or sketches. Secondary sources are based on primary sources, but are not written by people who were on the scene when an event took place. Ask students whether each of the following is a primary or secondary source:

Leonardo da Vinci's notebooks;

Self-portrait by Parmigianino;

The articles in this book.

Ask students to give examples of primary and secondary sources.

Have students practice the skill by completing the Activity Master.

Assessment Options

Questions

Use the following questions during individual conferences, or ask students to write the answers in their notebooks:

1 Why is the word *Renaissance* appropriate to describe the period between 1350 and the early 1600s?

2 How was the Renaissance spirit reflected in painting and sculpture?

3 How did the work of Renaissance scientists change the way people looked at the world?

4 Why was the invention of the printing press a turning point in history?

5 What role did Martin Luther play in the Reformation?

6 What were two important effects of the Reformation?

Assessment Activity

Have students work alone or in pairs to create a collage illustrating one of the three Big Ideas in "Renaissance." Students can use pictures from magazines, download images, or create their own illustrations. Each image should be captioned and the collage titled.

Collages should:

✓ accurately represent the Big Idea

✓ include images that support the Big Idea

✓ include clear and well-written captions

Multiple-choice Test

Use the multiple-choice test on page 81.

Home-school Connection

Students and their family members can discuss how beautifying a city affects the lives of its inhabitants. They can identify ways in which their own city has made life more pleasant—for example, by creating parks, building beautiful buildings, erecting statues and memorials, and so on—and compare these efforts with what was done in Florence, Venice and other European cities during the Renaissance.

Vocabulary: Relate Words

Part A: The words below have something to do with the Renaissance. In the circles, write a meaning for each word. On the lines, write a sentence that relates the word to the Renaissance.

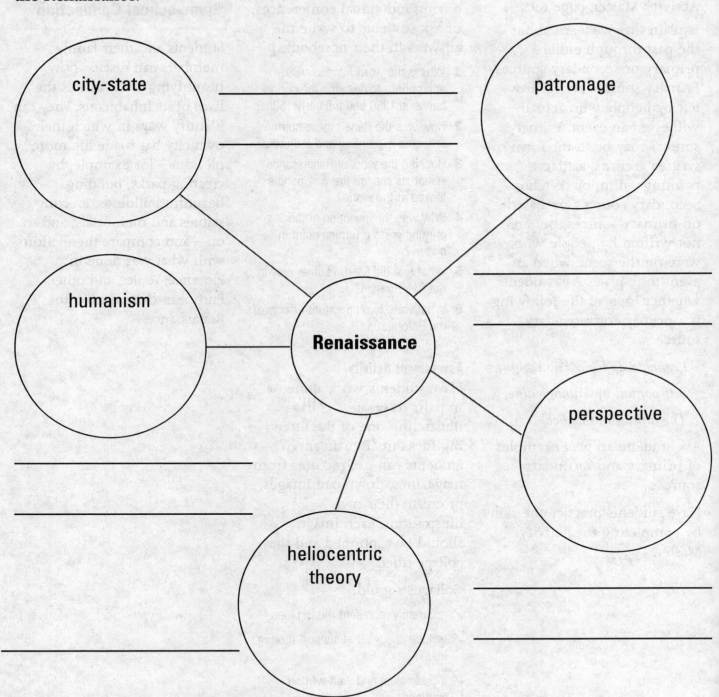

Part B: Draw the graphic above on a separate piece of paper and write *Reformation* in the center and these words in the circles: *heretic*; *indulgence*; *movable type*; *pope*; and *Protestant*. Give the meaning of each word and tell how it relates to the Reformation.

Read Strategically: Identify Problems and Solutions

As you read "New Styles in Art," you will explore problems Renaissance painters faced as they tried to create art that was different from what had been produced in the past. For each problem below, list one or more solutions that artists used in their search for "new" art.

1. Problem: To find new subject matter for painting

Solution(s): _____

_____

_____

_____

2. Problem: To make a flat surface appear to have three dimensions

Solution(s): _____

_____

_____

_____

3. Problem: To make some objects in the painting appear closer to the viewer than others

Solution(s): _____

_____

_____

_____

4. Problem: To blend color areas to create more natural-looking shades and forms

Solution(s): _____

_____

_____

_____

Read Strategically: Identify Cause-and-effect Relationships

As you read "The Book That Changed the World," think about the cause-and-effect relationships described in the article. A cause is the reason why something happened. An effect is what happens as a result. Write at least one cause for each effect described in the question.

1. Why did Gutenberg think that he could print books using individual letters cast out of hot metal?

_____

_____

2. Why did Gutenberg decide that the first book he would print on his printing press would be the Bible?

_____

_____

3. Why was printing the Bible such an enormous task?

_____

_____

4. Why did printing of the Bible mark the start of an explosion of book printing and learning?

_____

_____

5. Why did increasingly large numbers of people learn to read?

_____

_____

**This last question cannot be answered from information in this article.
You will need to draw a conclusion to answer it.**

6. Why might a Bible that anyone could read—written in a person's own language rather than Latin—pose a challenge to the Church?

_____

_____

Investigate World History: Use a Primary Source Document

A primary source is an on-the-spot description of an event, or a statement made by someone who lived at the time an event occurred. The excerpt below was written by Vignero, a friend of Michelangelo. Read the excerpt and answer the questions that follow.

I may add that I have seen Michael Angelo [Michelangelo], although then sixty years old and not in robust health, strike more chips from the hardest marble in a quarter of an hour than would be carried off by three stonecutters in three or four times as long. . . He would approach the marble with such impetuosity [passion], not to say fury, that I have often thought the whole work must be dashed to pieces. At one blow he would strike off pieces of three or four inches; yet with such exactitude was each stroke given that a mere atom more would sometimes have spoiled the whole work.

—from James Harvey Robinson, *Readings in European History*

1. How can you tell that this is a primary source?

_____

_____

2. Based on this excerpt, how would you describe Michelangelo at this time in his life?

_____

_____

3. What are Vignero's impressions of Michelangelo as a sculptor?

_____

_____

4. What conclusions can you draw about Michelangelo from this excerpt?

_____

_____

Overview of Titles
教学目标

World History	Focus on Nonfiction		Focus on Social Studies
	Title	**Text Features**	**Social Studies Learning Objectives**
	Early Humans	• Expository text • Article titles and subheads • Contents, overview and notes • Illustrations and photographs with captions • Maps, time lines and sidebars	• Relate the importance of technology to early humans • Explain the role of art in a developing culture • Identify the stages that led to the formation of early cities • Describe processes and tools archaeologists use to learn about the past • Interpret a time line
	The First Civilizations	• Expository text • Article titles and subheads • Contents, overview and notes • Illustrations and photographs with captions	• Identify and locate the Fertile Crescent • Name the basic features of a civilization and cite examples from Sumerian and ancient Egyptian civilizations • Identify the relationship between growth of civilizations and geographical features • Explain how archaeologists study the past
	Greek Civilization	• Expository text • Article titles and subheads • Contents, overview and notes • Illustrations and photographs with captions • Maps, time lines and sidebars	• Explain effects of geography on a civilization • Compare the cultures of Athens and Sparta • Identify democratic features of Athenian government • Describe some classical features of Greek architecture • Use a primary source • Map the conquests of Alexander the Great
	Ancient Rome	• Expository text • Article titles and subheads • Contents, overview and notes • Illustrations and photographs with captions	• Analyze a time line • Trace routes on a map • Compare republican and authoritarian governments • Describe the importance of the system of Roman roads • Recognize some problems of an expanding empire • Cite examples of the Roman legacy
	The Middle Ages	• Expository text • Article titles and subheads • Contents, overview and notes • Illustrations and photographs with captions • Maps, time lines, sidebars	• Examine the role of the Church during the Middle Ages • Recognize importance of a city's location to trade • Describe work and life in a medieval town • Recognize the political importance of the Magna Carta • Explain why the Battle of Crécy was a turning point
	Renaissance	• Expository text • Article titles and subheads • Contents, overview and notes • Illustrations and photographs with captions • Maps, time lines and diagrams • Sidebars and features	• Explain why the Renaissance began in the Italian city-states • Compare Renaissance and pre-Renaissance artistic styles • Name some Renaissance scientists and explain their ideas or discoveries • Relate Martin Luther to the Reformation • Interpret a primary source

Communication Skills

Reading Skills and Strategies	Writing Skills	Listening and Speaking
• Identify main ideas and details • Distinguish fact from opinion • Use context clues • Sequence • Identify cause-and-effect relationships • Draw conclusions	• Prepare an interview guide • Write a script for a documentary film • Prepare an outline for a mystery story	• Broadcast a TV news story
• Identify problems and solutions • Distinguish fact from opinion • Relate words • Recognize cause-and-effect relationships • Identify main ideas and details • Sequence • Draw conclusions	• Write an original epic • Write a diary entry	• Present a skit • Role-play an interview • Debate a topic
• Compare and contrast • Make generalizations • Use word origins • Recognize cause-and-effect relationships • Identify main ideas and details • Summarize • Draw conclusions	• Create a myth • Write an obituary for a historical figure • Take notes for a TV script	• Debate an issue • Read aloud
• Identify main ideas and details • Identify problems and solutions • Relate words • Recognize cause-and-effect relationships • Use visuals to aid comprehension • Draw conclusions	• Write a report • Write a compare/contrast paragraph • Write an essay	• Read aloud
• Recognize cause-and-effect relationships • Identify main ideas and details • Relate words • Compare and contrast • Sequence • Summarize	• Write "A Day in the Life of a Medieval..." article • Write a descriptive paragraph • Create a page for an illuminated manuscript	• Give an oral presentation • Have a panel discussion
• Identify problems and solutions • Recognize cause-and-effect relationships • Relate words • Identify main ideas and details • Summarize • Sequence • Generalize	• Write a profile/biography • Create a travel brochure • Review a work of art	• Deliver a speech • Broadcast a news report

Visit the *Reading Expeditions* Website

www.ngschoolpub.org

Reading Expeditions has its own place on the National Geographic School Publishing website. Explore the online resources that support and extend this series. This site provides a variety of options to support your instruction, including teaching materials for specific titles and information on readability levels.

- **Comprehensive Teaching Notes and Activity Masters**

  The downloadable lesson notes for each title include a variety of teaching strategies. Additionally, for each title, you'll find printable blackline masters that develop literacy and content skills.

- **Assessment Materials**

  The online assessment materials will include a variety of tools for measuring students' developmental progress.

Keep checking the *Reading Expeditions* site for more new resources and for updates about additional titles to come.

Just log onto **www.ngschoolpub.org** and see how *Reading Expeditions* continues to grow.

Teacher's Guides

A number of excellent websites from educational organizations and government agencies provide helpful Internet resources. The following sites may assist you in preparation for your lessons.

International Reading Association (IRA)

http://www.reading.org

As stated on their website, the mission of the IRA is to "promote high levels of literacy for all." The website provides a wealth of reading research materials, conference information, and articles from journals and other publications.

U.S. Department of Education

http://www.ed.gov

This website offers an ever-growing collection of information about the Department, including the latest news about educational programs, policies and legislation, grant opportunities, publications, and research and statistics. The site also includes special collections of information for parents, teachers and students.

Educational Resources Information Center (ERIC)

http://www.eric.ed.gov

ERIC is a national information system designed to provide ready access to an extensive body of education-related literature. The database offers the world's largest source of education information, providing a variety of services and products.

Literacy Matters

http://www.literacymatters.org/content/socialstudies.htm

This site is housed at the Education Development Center (EDC) in Newton, MA, a nonprofit education and health organization. The site offers social studies teachers help in integrating literacy strategies into their content area teaching as well as links to other sites on literacy skills for the social studies classroom.

National Council for the Social Studies (NCSS)

http://www.socialstudies.org/classroom

In addition to providing current education news and legislative updates the NCSS site includes updated lists of new classroom resources, lesson plans, and suggestions for teachable moments linking current events to World History standards-based content.

National Geographic

http://www.nationalgeographic.com

From the main site for the National Geographic Society, students can link to a huge collection of resources including maps, journals of expeditions, online archives of *National Geographic* magazine, and photographs. They can also access the home page of the Reading Expeditions program.

Although one purpose of assessment is to measure performance so that results can be shared with parents and school administrators, the primary purpose of assessment is to gather information to inform instruction. Assessment offers valuable insights into students' learning and allows teachers to plan instruction that supports and challenges students. It deals with both the knowledge students attain as well as the process of learning.

A variety of assessment tools are available with *Reading Expeditions.*

Discussion Questions

For each title in *Reading Expeditions,* a series of discussion questions are provided in the Teacher's Guide (See **Assessment Options: Questions**). These questions tap into students' understanding of the information in the text and invite students to use the text to make connections, draw conclusions, and make generalizations. The questions can be used in individual reading conferences, or students can write responses in their reading notebooks. In evaluating student responses, you may want to use the following rubric.

Questions

Use the following questions during individual conferences, or ask students to write the answers in their notebooks:

1 Why did cities develop in the Fertile Crescent and the Nile Valley?

2 How was cuneiform used in the ancient Middle East?

3 What were the purposes of Hammurabi's Code?

4 How did the Egyptians prepare for death?

5 What can technology such as X-rays reveal about life in Mesopotamia and ancient Egypt?

Teacher's Guide page 25 for "The First Civilizations"

Rubric for Evaluating Responses

4	Answer addresses all parts of the question and shows sound reasoning, with appropriate examples drawn from the text to support conclusions and inferences.
3	Answer addresses most parts of the question and shows inferential thinking in filling in unstated connections. There may be some omissions or minor errors of fact.
2	Answer does not deal directly with the question but may deal with some related aspect of the question. The response reflects a literal understanding of the text but shows little inferential comprehension of the information in the text.
1	Answer shows little comprehension of the question or the text. It may be unrelated or inappropriate.

Multiple-choice Tests

A multiple-choice test is offered for each title in *World History*. The tests appear on pages 76-81 of this guide. The comprehension and vocabulary tests offer a quick assessment of basic understandings of the text. Questions in the test cover the key ideas and concept words presented in the title and provide students with practice in taking multiple-choice tests.

Assessment Activity

For each title in *World History*, there is an Assessment Activity provided in the teaching notes (See **Assessment Options: Assessment Activity**). This activity outlines an alternative performance-based assessment option in which students can make a product or give a performance that demonstrates an understanding of the text. This alternative assessment can provide insight into how well the student understands and applies the knowledge learned from the text.

For each Assessment Activity, an evaluation checklist is provided to help measure performance against defined criteria. These checklists typically address both the content and the execution of the assessment product. Clearly defined criteria make it easier to give an objective evaluation of the activity.

In addition, you may want to record anecdotal notes that give insight into such skills as problem solving and collaboration.

Performance-based assessments are especially useful with students for whom paper-and-pencil activities do not reflect the student's learning. These activities can tap into special skills that are often overlooked by traditional assessment tools.

Name: _____

Early Humans

Circle the letter of the correct answer.

1. The most important trend during the Neolithic Revolution was that early humans

   a. learned to hunt animals and gather wild plants.

   b. began to make simple stone weapons.

   c. changed from hunter-gatherers to food producers.

   d. died out as ice sheets covered the Earth.

2. Today, scientists view the Neandertals as

   a. direct ancestors of humans.

   b. "apelike" and dumb brutes.

   c. having an organized society.

   d. the first humans to have animals as companion.

3. Permanent settlements began when

   a. humans were able to plant and gather a steady supply of food.

   b. aurochs and other animals died out.

   c. the human population increased.

   d. humans learned to trade with other communities.

4. Archaeologists use carbon 14 to

   a. keep a record of the artifacts they have unearthed.

   b. prepare an artifact for X-ray or CT scan.

   c. distinguish between living and non-living objects.

   d. determine the age of artifacts or other remains.

5. Bones found on the Channel Islands off the coast of California suggest that

   a. the Clovis people came from Monte Verde.

   b. early Americans may have used boats to travel to the Americas.

   c. there are more Clovis sites to be found in the West than in the East.

   d. there was no land bridge from Siberia to Alaska.

Write the letter of the correct definition next to each word.

_____ **6.** artisan

_____ **7.** flint

_____ **8.** archeologist

_____ **9.** mammoth

_____ **10.** prehistory

   a. extinct type of elephant that lived during the Ice Age

   b. period of human past before writing was invented

   c. fine-grained quartz used to make tools

   d. person skilled in a craft or trade

   e. scientist who studies the remains of past cultures

Name: _____

The First Civilizations

Circle the letter of the correct answer.

1. Cuneiform was important because it was

   a. the first written code of laws.

   b. a written language used to keep records.

   c. the world's first great work of literature.

   d. the first school for boys.

2. According to Hammurabi's Code

   a. the punishment should match the crime.

   b. all laws apply equally to everyone.

   c. consumers had no protection or rights.

   d. only the king could set prison sentences.

3. The annual flooding of the Nile left behind

   a. strong currents, which made river transportation impossible.

   b. silt, which renewed the soil.

   c. tall reeds called papyrus.

   d. canals, which brought water to the planted fields.

4. To build the Great Pyramid of Giza,

   a. engineers had to follow the steps listed in the *Book of the Dead.*

   b. workers had to travel between their distant homes and Giza each day.

   c. farmers were forced to become slaves.

   d. teams of workers tackled different parts of the project.

5. Preparations for a pharaoh's death began long before he died because

   a. Egypt's well-being depended on the pharaoh surviving in the afterlife.

   b. servants had to be mummified before the pharaoh died.

   c. priests had to decide which pyramid would serve as a tomb.

   d. the king of the dead, Osiris, demanded many years' preparation.

Write the letter of the correct definition next to each word.

_____ **6.** archaeologist

_____ **7.** delta

_____ **8.** expedition

_____ **9.** hieroglyphics

_____ **10.** stylus

   a. land at a river's mouth

   b. picture writing of ancient Egypt

   c. scientist who studies the remains of peoples and cultures

   d. sharp, pointed tool for writing

   e. trip taken for a specific purpose

Name: _____

Greek Civilization

Circle the letter of the correct answer.

1. Why did the ancient Greeks become a seafaring people?

  a. They liked to eat fish, particularly thunnos.

  b. There was little flat land for farming.

  c. They were expert shipbuilders.

  d. They wanted to please Poseidon, god of the sea.

2. Which is NOT among the legacies of ancient Greece?

  a. The *Illiad*, a long poem about the Trojan War, by Homer.

  b. Advice from the oracle at Apollo's shrine at Delphi.

  c. The Olympic Games, which celebrated strength, stamina and athletic skill.

  d. The ideas of democracy, which began in Athens.

3. Which of these statements best describes the Spartans?

  a. They valued the arts and freedom of thought.

  b. They built large outdoor theaters and beautiful buildings such as the Parthenon.

  c. They did not welcome outsiders and became skilled at providing for themselves.

  d. They were lawless and weak.

4. In which way was democracy in Athens limited?

  a. Only male citizens older than 18 could vote.

  b. Athens was ruled by a king.

  c. Only the Council could propose laws.

  d. Only citizens could consult the priests at Delphi.

5. Which of these people believed that illness had a logical, physical explanation?

  a. Socrates.   **b.** Alexander.

  c. Hippocrates.   **d.** Pericles.

Write the letter of the correct definition next to each word.

_____ **6.** ostracism   **a.** rapidly spreading disease, often causing death

_____ **7.** logic   **b.** the upper class in society

_____ **8.** plague   **c.** exile of a person thought to be an enemy of the state

_____ **9.** colony   **d.** method of correct reasoning

_____ **10.** aristocracy   **e.** region controlled by another country

Multiple-choice Test

Ancient Rome

Circle the letter of the correct answer.

1. The Roman Army did all of the following EXCEPT

   a. fight as gladiators.

   b. build roads and bridges when they were not fighting.

   c. spread Roman culture throughout the provinces.

   d. serve in their legion for 16 to 26 years.

2. The economy and prosperity of ancient Roman depended on its

   a. large, beautiful buildings.

   b. "bread and circuses."

   c. vast network of roads.

   d. location on the Mediterranean Sea.

3. The reign of Julius Caesar marked the

   a. beginning of Christianity.

   b. defeat of Carthage.

   c. division of the empire into eastern and western parts.

   d. end of the Roman Republic.

4. One reason why Christianity spread so quickly was that

   a. the Roman emperor Nero allowed freedom of religion.

   b. Christian worship was the same as Roman worship.

   c. missionaries spread word of the faith.

   d. the Romans persecuted nonbelievers.

5. The Colosseum in Rome was built as a place where

   a. legionnaires could practice their fighting skills.

   b. the Roman Senate could meet.

   c. the Romans could worship their gods.

   d. gladiators fought wild beasts.

Write the letter of the correct definition next to each word.

_____ **6.** vault

_____ **7.** dictator

_____ **8.** forum

_____ **9.** aqueduct

_____ **10.** republic

a. channel used to carry water

b. public meeting place

c. government in which citizens elect their leaders

d. curved, archlike ceiling

e. Roman leader with complete power in emergencies

Name: _____

The Middle Ages

Circle the letter of the correct answer.

1. Constantinople became the richest city in the medieval world because of its

   a. many beautiful cathedrals.

   b. geographic location.

   c. secret weapon called "Greek fire."

   d. economy based on money, not land.

2. As a result of an increase in both population and trade,

   a. the middle class lost power.

   b. the Silk Roads were abandoned.

   c. a strong, central government was set up.

   d. cities and towns grew, attracting many people from the farmlands.

3. The spread of the Black Death throughout Europe resulted in

   a. declining trade and deserted farms.

   b. the growth of monasteries.

   c. the outbreak of the Hundred Years War.

   d. a more powerful Church.

4. The main purpose of the Magna Carta was to

   a. limit the king's power and guarantee the rights of his subjects.

   b. give men and women equal rights and responsibilities.

   c. establish a national government and identify its rules.

   d. raise taxes to wage war against the French.

5. The alchemists are viewed as scientific pioneers because they

   a. could change substances into gold.

   b. translated Arab documents to learn about science.

   c. began the process of observation and experimentation.

   d. were skilled teachers and learned men.

Write the letter of the correct definition next to each word or term.

_____ **6.** plague

_____ **7.** feudal

_____ **8.** chivalry

_____ **9.** guild

_____ **10.** siege

   a. code of conduct for knights

   b. association of workers in a particular craft

   c. epidemic disease

   d. military tactic of cutting the enemy off from outside assistance

   e. society in which the landowners held power

Name: _____

Renaissance

Circle the letter of the correct answer.

1. How did the ruling families throughout Italy help foster the Renaissance?

  a. They recommended reforms in the Catholic Church.

  b. They provided economic help to thinkers and artists.

  c. They financed the building of fleets of galleys for trade.

  d. They staged many elaborate city pageants.

2. How did Renaissance painters achieve greater realism in their paintings?

  a. They used egg-based paints which dried quickly.

  b. They stopped blending colors.

  c. They used perspective to give the appearance of depth.

  d. They painting only religious subjects.

3. Why was Leonardo da Vinci considered a "Renaissance Man"?

  a. He kept detailed notebooks.

  b. He set up his own workshop.

  c. He painted *The Last Supper* and the *Mona Lisa*.

  d. He could do many different things well.

4. Which of the following scientific theories was developed during the Renaissance?

  a. The sun is the center of the universe.

  b. The planets orbit around the Earth.

  c. The heavier the object, the faster it falls.

  d. The heavens were made up of pure spheres of light.

5. What events occurred as a result of Martin Luther's protest?

  a. Elizabeth I was crowned queen in England.

  b. The printing press was invented and an explosion of learning followed.

  c. The Holy Roman Empire was formed.

  d. New religions developed and reforms were made in the Catholic Church.

Write the letter of the correct definition next to each word or term.

_____ **6.** heretic   **a.** Renaissance viewpoint celebrating human freedom

_____ **7.** patronage   **b.** shallow body of water separated from the sea

_____ **8.** doge   **c.** person whose beliefs go against the teachings of an established church

_____ **9.** humanism   **d.** power of appointing people to government or political positions

_____ **10.** lagoon   **e.** ruler of Venice

Answers to Multiple-choice Tests

World History

Early Humans

1. c	6. d
2. c	7. c
3. a	8. e
4. d	9. a
5. b	10. b

Ancient Rome

1. a	6. d
2. c	7. e
3. d	8. b
4. c	9. a
5. d	10. c

The First Civilizations

1. b	6. c
2. a	7. a
3. b	8. e
4. d	9. b
5. a	10. d

The Middle Ages

1. b	6. c
2. d	7. e
3. a	8. a
4. a	9. b
5. c	10. d

Greek Civilization

1. b	6. c
2. b	7. d
3. c	8. a
4. a	9. e
5. c	10. b

Renaissance

1. b	6. c
2. c	7. d
3. d	8. e
4. a	9. a
5. d	10. b

Using Graphic Organizers
运用图表

Graphic organizers are visual representations of information. They can be used to help assess students' understanding of informational text as well as their ability to communicate information in different ways. Graphic organizers are important because they help students to comprehend, summarize and synthesize complex ideas and information.

The books in the *Reading Expeditions World History* series cover a wide variety of cultural topics. Graphic organizers are excellent tools to help examine these complex issues as students reconstruct and process the information presented in the text.

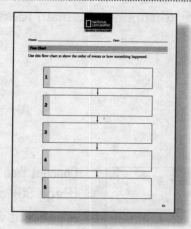

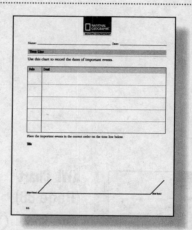

Flow Chart
(Page 85)

The flow chart is an effective tool to represent a sequence of events or steps in a process. This graphic can show the order of particular events in a historical era or a person's life as well as show cause-and-effect relationships.

Time Line
(Page 86)

A time line is an effective graphic representation that chronologically maps events across a period of time. Time lines are useful in tracking the order of historical events.

Students can fill in the dates of significant events in the development of an individual or a civilization.

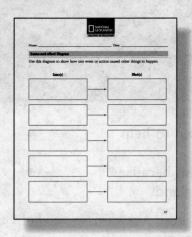

Cause-and-effect Diagram
(Page 87)

Cause-and-effect diagrams show causal relationships among actions and events. They can show how one or more actions or events affect subsequent events.

Understanding cause-and-effect relationships helps students to understand *why* things happen and *what* happens as a result.

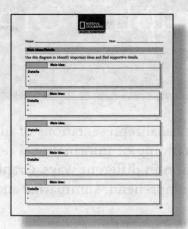

Main Ideas/Details
(Page 89)

The main ideas-details graphic organizer helps readers to first identify the important ideas or concepts presented in an article, or section and then find supportive details. This visual gives students practice in outlining information and in recognizing the author's hierarchy of importance as well as the support the author builds to support the main ideas.

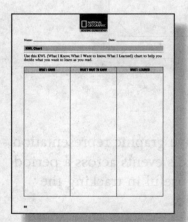

KWL Chart
(Page 88)

The KWL (What I **K**now, What I **W**ant to Know, What I **L**earned) chart provides a graphic means for students to explore their prior knowledge about a subject, set a purpose for their reading based on that prior knowledge, and compare the knowledge they gained from their reading to that prior knowledge.

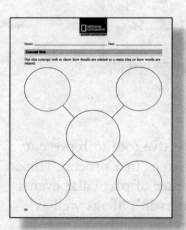

Concept Web
(Page 90)

A concept web is a useful visual for showing a variety of relationships. Concept webs are well suited to show the main idea and supporting details. They can also be used to show how vocabulary words relate to the theme or topic of a book or article.

Concept webs often show one main circle with several secondary circles as spokes off the center. Youu may wish to add secondary circles to the concept web provided on page 90 to reflect the content or vocabulary of specific titles.

Name: _____ Date: _____

Flow Chart

Use this flow chart to show the order of events or how something happened.

1	

↓

2	

↓

3	

↓

4	

↓

5	

Name: _____ Date: _____

Time Line

Use this chart to record the dates of important events.

Date	Event

Place the important events in the correct order on the time line below.

Title _____

(Start Date) _____ (End Date)

Name: _____ Date: _____

Cause-and-effect Diagram

Use this diagram to show how one event or action caused other things to happen.

Cause(s)   **Effect(s)**

Name: _____ Date: _____

KWL Chart

Use this KWL (What I **K**now, What I **W**ant to know, What I **L**earned) chart to help you decide what you want to learn as you read.

WHAT I KNOW	WHAT I WANT TO KNOW	WHAT I LEARNED

Name: _____ Date: _____

Main Ideas/Details

Use this diagram to identify important ideas and find supportive details.

Main Idea:	
Details	
•	
•	

Main Idea:	
Details	
•	
•	

Main Idea:	
Details	
•	
•	

Main Idea:	
Details	
•	
•	

Main Idea:	
Details	
•	
•	

Name: _____   Date: _____

Concept Web

Use this concept web to show how details are related to a main idea or how words are related.

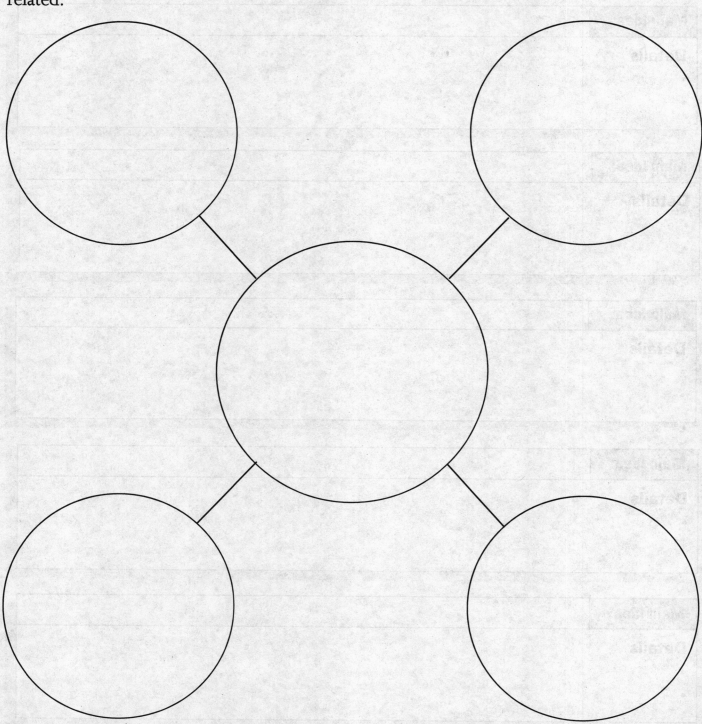

Notes